SAINT FRANCIS

SAINT FRANCIS
OF ASSISI

JOHN R. H. MOORMAN
Bishop of Ripon

LONDON

SPCK

First published in 1950 by SCM Press

First published by SPCK in 1963
New edition 1976

SPCK
Holy Trinity Church
Marylebone Road, London NW1 4DU

Made and printed in Great Britain by
The Camelot Press Ltd, Southampton

ISBN 0 281 02946 6

Contents

Abbreviations Used in the Notes

Opusc.   *Opuscula S. Francisci*, ed. Quaracchi, 1904.

Sac. Com.   *Sacrum Commercium*, or *The Converse of Francis and his Sons with Holy Poverty*, Temple Classics, 1904.

Per.   *Legenda Antiqua S. Francisci*, ed. F. Delorme, in *La France Franciscaine*, 1926.

1 Cel.   *First Life of S. Francis* by Thomas of Celano, translated by A. G. Ferrers Howell, 1908.

2 Cel.   *Second Life of S. Francis* by Thomas of Celano, translated by A. G. Ferrers Howell, 1908.

3 Soc.   *The Legend of S. Francis* by the Three Companions, translated by Salter, Temple Classics, 1905.

Spec.   *Speculum Perfectionis* or *The Mirror of Perfection*, translated by Sebastian Evans, 1898.

Bon:

Leg. Maj.	*Legenda S. Francisci* by S. Bonaventura, translated by E. G. S(alter), Temple Classics, 1904.
Fior.	*Fioretti*, or *The Little Flowers of S. Francis*. Various translations and editions.
Chron. Jordani	*Chronica Fratris Jordani*, ed. Boehmer, 1908.
A New Fior.	*A New Fioretti*, a Collection of Assisi hitherto untranslated, ed. J. R. H. Moorman, 1946.

Preface to the New Edition

It is interesting to note that the first Life of Saint Francis to be written in English appeared in the year 1870. It was written by Mrs Oliphant, a prolific writer of history books and novels which flowed from her pen at the rate of about five volumes a year. Yet this was a scholarly work, based on the medieval Latin sources, but written in a style which would appeal to the serious-minded reader of mid-Victorian England.

Since then much has happened, and books about St Francis have poured from the presses of Europe and America. Nor does the demand seem to grow any less, as people turn again and again to that remarkable man whose significance in the history of the Church we have at last begun to recognize.

Francis has obviously something to say to people of all kinds. He was a mystic with a special interest in, and understanding of, nature. He was a poet, the first to write verse in any modern language. He was a man of great courage, risking his life in carrying out his ideals. He inspired large numbers of men to give away all that they possessed and live as vagabonds, begging their bread from door to door.

All these things were important, and all combine to make him a very remarkable man. But perhaps the thing about him which appeals to us most today is the challenge which he threw down to the standards and values of the ordinary, secular life of man. In our own age, when wealth, comfort, and security are so often regarded as the best things which a man can have, Francis deliberately abandoned all of these things, even regarding them as evils which must, at all costs, be fought against and avoided. He would not allow any of his followers to accept, or even to touch, money. He sought out the hard, rough, comfortless places of the world in which to live. He took no thought for the morrow, prepared to die of cold or hunger, if it was the will of God that he should do so.

Francis has, undoubtedly, a very special message to those of us who live in a highly materialistic world where money is so often regarded as the only criterion of contentment. We need, therefore, to look at St Francis, especially at things like the chapter in *The Little Flowers* on 'Perfect Joy', to see how false this is (below, pp. 34–6). The call of St Francis was not to escape from the world, but to give oneself to the world, asking nothing for oneself and ready to suffer and to die for the souls of men.

So I send forth again, after twenty-six years, this short life of that great and holy man, that devoted disciple of Christ, the one whom Renan called 'the one perfect Christian', in the hope that his message will continue to be heard, understood, and put into practice in the ways best suited to the world in which we now live.

JOHN R. H. MOORMAN

Durham 1976

1

Vocation

THE year 1206 seems to have marked the real turning-point in the life of Francesco Bernardone. Up till then he had lived the life of a gay young man, well endowed with natural abilities and the long purse of a rich father, popular, pleasure-loving, and irresponsible. But in that year, at the age of four-and-twenty, his whole life was changed. Most of the things which he had formerly loved and valued he now despised, and the things which he had previously most disliked, became his most cherished possessions. Within a few months the dashing young man of Assisi had become a tramp, going about the town in rags and begging his food from door to door.

This remarkable change or conversion was brought about by a series of divine strokes or visitations, the first of which occurred when Francis was just at the point of achieving the greatest ambition of his youth. The son of rich, middle-class parents he had been brought up to enjoy life at their expense and to associate as far as possible with the nobility of the town. This Francis did well enough, for he was irrepressibly gay, naturally popular, and delightfully extravagant. The entertainments which he provided were fully appreciated by those who were lucky enough to be invited to them, while the charm of the host made him an acknowledged leader, even among men who were socially his superiors. Some later writers, in describing Francis' youth, have hinted at dark and nameless sins. Thomas of Celano, for example, writes of him " surpassing all his coevals in his bad progress in vanity" and as "an instigator of evil deeds";[1] but there is little evidence for this. Celano, no

[1] 1 *Cel.* 2.

doubt, was anxious to draw as sharp a contrast as possible between Francis' wayward youth and the purity of his later life. But if we look at the records of his early life there is really very little on which to build up such a theory. That he was vain and ostentatious there is no doubt. His clothes were made of the very best materials (his father being a cloth-merchant who had access to the finest fabrics in Europe) and no doubt they were sometimes over-flamboyant and sometimes a bit whimsical. Some of the citizens of Assisi spoke afterwards of his clothes being "beyond measure sumptuous" and one remembered a suit of his which he had had made partly of the richest cloth and partly of the cheapest and meanest, as a bright young man of to-day might go out to dinner in a white waistcoat and corduroys. But such youthful follies hardly deserve the name of "evil deeds".

Apart from these extravagances the picture which the early records give us of Francis' youth is that of a very charming and generous boy. He seems, even from early days, to have had a real sympathy with the poor, and would sometimes give most lavishly to them. He also had a real concern for the lonely and unpopular and unlovable, and hated suffering in any form, his natural gaiety being outraged at the sight of another who was unable to share in it. In 1202, when Francis was just entering manhood, he joined in a skirmish between the men of Assisi and the men of Perugia at the village of Ponte San Giovanni, the outcome of which was that he spent a year as a captive in some Perugian prison. Here, among his fellow prisoners, was one unhappy soul who made himself thoroughly unpopular with his fellows and was consequently ostracized by them. Francis could not endure this. Life in prison was bad enough: it became intolerable if there was to be disharmony among the fellow prisoners. So he went out of his way to be friendly to the outcast and in the end succeeded in making the peace.[1]

When the Perugians were sorting out their prisoners after the battle Francis presented a peculiar problem. Knights were

[1] 3 *Soc.* 4.

2

entitled to special terms, but Francis was not one of them. He was not a knight; but it was the ambition of his life to become one. The life of adventure and romance appealed very strongly to him, the thought of his being perhaps able to fight against tyranny or injustice or heresy he found most agreeable, while the picture of a knight-in-armour on a richly caparisoned horse would naturally appeal to his love of display. He therefore began now to look out for an opportunity of achieving his ambition.

The opportunity came in the year 1205 when a certain Count Gentile began to organize a party of young men from Assisi to go with him to join the armies of Walter of Brienne who was fighting on the Pope's behalf in the south of Italy. Walter was a popular figure who had captured the imagination of young men all over the country. His cause, too, was popular, for it represented the deepest feelings of the Italian people—their nationalism and their religious loyalty. So when Gentile made it known in Assisi that he was raising troops to go to the assistance of the Pope, Francis jumped at the opportunity. Preparations were immediately put in hand for his departure, his ambitious parents fully approving of a plan which might raise the social status of the family, and being quite prepared to spend almost unlimited sums of money on the equipment necessary to make a fine showing. When at last the day of their departure dawned, Francis excelled everyone in the magnificence of his attire, though he slightly chilled the ardour of his parents by suddenly and quite recklessly giving away his fine armour to a poor knight, who cut a sorry figure by the side of the resplendent tradesman. However, alternative supplies were soon found, and Francis rode out of the city in high hopes, a splendid figure dedicated to a splendid cause.

On the first evening the party slept at Spoleto, about thirty miles from Assisi, and it was here that Francis received the first of the divine strokes or visitations that were about to change his whole life. During the night, while he was half-asleep and half-awake, he became aware of a voice asking him

3

where he was going. When Francis had explained the purpose of his journey the voice said: "Which can do better for you, the lord or the servant?" Francis had no hesitation in saying, "The lord". "Why then", said the other, "do you leave the lord for the servant, and a rich lord for a poor?" Francis, mystified by this and groping for guidance, cried, "Lord, what wouldst thou have me do?" and the voice replied: "Return to your own country and you will be told what to do."[1]

Here was a crisis. Francis had ridden out of his home town amid the cheers of the people; how could he face going back, alone, to endure mockery and the accusation which young men most fear—the charge of cowardice? Some would think that he was afraid, some would say that he was homesick, many would believe that under all the finery and display lay a coward's heart. But the voice which had spoken in his conscience had about it a compulsion which could not be denied. All night Francis lay awake, tormented by this dilemma; but by dawn his mind was made up. Whatever the strange message meant it was clear that he must obey; and when his fellow travellers rose in the morning Francis had gone.

The return to Assisi must have been the hardest ordeal which Francis had yet had to face. Parents, neighbours, and all the riff-raff of the town would despise him and laugh at him. And how could he justify himself? He was not ill; there had been no call from home; how could he convey to them the urgency and compulsion of the message which he had received? As Francis rode back up the broad valley to his home town his heart must have been sore and his mind full of strange, conflicting thoughts. Only one thing was clear, and that was that, however great the cost might be, he could not have done otherwise.

Thus Francis endured the first of the series of divine strokes or visitations. In the account of the Spoletan incident and of what it led to we see the first sign of self-conquest, the first step in renunciation, the first mark of absolute submission to the Divine Will in the soul of this sensitive and ambitious

[1] 3 *Soc.* 6.

young man. God has made his first assault on Francis' defences, and the first crack has been made in them.

In spite of the collapse of the Apulian expedition Francis appears to have been as popular as ever with the youth of Assisi. Whatever scar the whole incident may have left on his own sensitive nature, it did not affect his relations with his friends. The gay life was resumed; parties, revels, and festivities were held; and Francis was soon back in his old place as acknowledged leader of every escapade, throwing his money about freely and constantly devising new forms of entertainment. The strange fiasco of the knightly enterprise was soon forgotten; Francis appeared to be as gay and radiant and irresponsible as ever.

Love, however, was still tracking him down. Little, perhaps, though Francis knew it, the message which he had heard at Spoleto had been no illusion. In answer to the first part of that message he had returned to his own country; the time was at hand when the second part of the message would be driven home and he would receive his instructions as to what he was to do.

The second stroke occurred on one of those uproarious evenings when Francis had plunged into the gay life and had been popularly elected as "master of the revels". The young men of Assisi, having had their feast, were parading through the streets of the city with Francis bringing up the rear, carrying his wand of office. Suddenly, in the words of the chronicler, he was "visited of the Lord". On this occasion the divine visitation seems to have rendered him totally immobile for, describing the affair afterwards, he said that, "had he been pricked as with knives all over at once, he could not have moved from the spot". There he stood, dressed in his gayest clothes and bearing his wand of office, alone in the middle of the road while his companions, not knowing what had happened, went noisily onwards. Eventually they discovered that their "master of the revels" was missing and went back to look for him. They found him still in a trance-like state, and, assuming that such behaviour could proceed only from one cause, they asked him: "Are you in love, Francis?" "Yes," he replied, "I am in love with a bride nobler, richer, and fairer than you have ever seen."[1] Such a reply could only be received with laughter, and the incident was quickly forgotten. But not by Francis.

Who was the bride? The chroniclers say that the bride was "True Religion, nobler, richer, and fairer than others in her poverty"; but that is perhaps too simple an explanation. Francis was already wedded to Religion of a kind, but this second visitation shook him far more violently than his former experience at Spoleto. There he had conversed with the voice and received his orders; this time he was struck dumb and almost senseless by the violence of the stroke so that his companions were mystified and fearful when they returned to him. Whether, on this occasion, there was any voice speaking to him is not recorded, but it is clear that some message was forced upon him, so cogent and so compulsive that it changed the whole course of his life.

I think there can be little doubt that "the bride" was Poverty. Possibly, as they paraded through the streets, Francis' attention may have been caught by the sight of some poor beggar settling down to sleep in an archway while the rich young men, well fed and well dressed, went home to their comfortable beds. At any rate Francis seems, at the moment of this spiritual experience, to have been overwhelmed by the thought of Poverty not as an enemy or as a nightmare, but as an ideal to be achieved by great personal effort. Francis had been brought up in a rich home and, though his mother appears to have been a kindly and affectionate creature, his father was obviously a hard man of business. The atmosphere in which Francis had lived and the teaching which he must have absorbed was that man's chief end in life was to do well for himself. Poverty was a terrible thing, like a quicksand, into which a man might fall through misfortune or carelessness.

[1] 3 *Soc.* 7.

It was an ugly thing, attended only by coarseness and dirt and squalor. It was to be avoided like the plague.

In a flash Francis saw the falsehood in all this. Far from being an evil and terrible thing poverty was the handmaid of Christ who "chose a poor and humble lot" and deliberately associated with the poor and the outcast and the squalid. Gradually Francis built up a new theory about Poverty, investing it with all the attributes of a great and beautiful lady of the kind whom any knight dreamed about and hoped one day to rescue from distress and make his own. The elaboration of the theme came later, but the sudden divine visitation in the streets of Assisi seems to have revealed to Francis a great truth which he was destined to spend the rest of his life in making known to the world.

The effect of this experience was twofold. In the first place Francis now began to withdraw more and more from the rowdy, pleasure-seeking life which he had led, and to spend far more time in quiet meditation and prayer. Secondly, he now exhibited a far keener interest in the poor, and went out of his way to give lavishly and recklessly whenever he could. "Whenever any poor man asked him an alms out of doors," say the chroniclers, "he would supply him with money if he could; had he no ready money, he would give him his cap or girdle rather than send the poor man empty away. And if it were that he had naught of this kind, he would go to some hidden place, and strip off his shirt, and send the poor man thither that he might take it unto himself for the sake of God." He also used to buy ornaments and vessels for the church and send them to poor priests, or he would lay the table as if for a large company and then take all the food out into the streets and distribute it to the poor. All his thoughts now seemed to be turned to the poor and to be absorbed with the question of Poverty.[1]

Shortly afterwards he had an opportunity of going a step further and of discovering for himself what it felt like to be destitute. He had gone on a pilgrimage to Rome, where at

[1] 3 *Soc.* 8.

the shrine of St Peter, he was horrified at the meagre contributions of his fellow pilgrims, and in his reckless way he pulled out his purse and flung it through the grating of the altar with such a crash that everyone in the church turned to stare. Such an act was typical of Francis who loved recklessness and hated anything mean or parsimonious or calculating. But it presented an immediate problem. He had thrown all his ready money away; how was he to pay for his next meal?

So, driven perhaps more by necessity than by any conscious desire for a new experience, he determined to beg for his food among the crowd of seedy-looking, whining beggars who crowded round the doors of the great church. Somehow or other he prevailed upon one of the beggars to lend him his rags and for a few hours the fastidious Assisian youth might have been seen in the filthy, lousy rags of a beggar, crying out in bad French for pity while a few kind folk tossed him a coin or two.[1] When all was over Francis returned to Assisi. But he had learnt something at Rome. For a little while he had stood on equal footing with the poor. He had conquered his repulsion and had forced himself to lay on his clean limbs the squalid rags of a beggar, and for a short time to identify himself with the dregs of society, the very people whom he had been taught to hate and despise.

The adventure at Rome had been hard, but a harder ordeal lay before him in his own town. By these experiments in poverty he was learning step by step, to accept a totally new attitude towards the poor. If hitherto they had been merely objects of commiseration, the proper recipients of small alms which cost little and could be so easily thrown to them, he was now beginning to regard them as in a special way dear to Christ and therefore of all people the most honourable and the most lovable. As he stood begging on the steps of St Peter's his heart was warmed with the thought that he was standing among the friends of Christ and for a moment might be counted as one of them. But there were more repulsive people in the world than the poor, even the poor who crawled

[1] 3 Soc. 10.

out of the filthy slums of medieval Rome. Of all the loathsome sights there was nothing to equal that of the lepers. Practically uncared-for, many of them were left to rot to death in the foul lazarettos scattered up and down the country. One of these lay close to Assisi, and so much did the young Francis dread the chance of an encounter with a leper that he carefully avoided going anywhere near it, while the stench which rose from it would make him cover his nose, so nauseating was it.

One day, about this time, while riding close to Assisi he met a leper. He would undoubtedly have put spurs to his horse and galloped away had he not realized that here was another and more searching test of his new attitude towards the poor. For a moment the two men were brought face to face while the angels looked down to see what the new disciple of Christ would do. Would love win? Would the great Christian virtues of compassion and charity be able to overcome fear and disgust? Francis was facing, at that moment, what was perhaps the hardest test of his whole life. But he did not hesitate. Dismounting from his horse he walked up to the leper, gave him an alms, and then, slowly and deliberately, kissed his hand.[1]

Love had won, but at a price. As the *Legend of the Three Companions* says: he had to "do violence unto himself". He had to fight down his pride, his squeamishness, his horror, as he saw before him this wreck of humanity and knew that he must press the man's rotten flesh against his lips. From that point Francis never looked back. A day or two later he visited the leper-house and went round to each of the sufferers, kissing his hand and placing a coin in it. Never again did he flinch from contact with a leper, but the struggle had been a hard one. When Francis came to write his testament, shortly before his death, he realized that the overcoming of his natural shrinking from the lepers had been the real turning-point of his life. His will opens with these words: "The Lord gave to me, Brother Francis, thus to begin to do penance. For when I was in sin it seemed very bitter to me to see lepers, and the Lord Himself led me among them, and I showed mercy to

[1] 3 *Soc.* II.

9

them. And when I left them, what had seemed to me bitter was changed into sweetness of body and soul."[1]

In these words Francis admits that he had had a struggle but he also suggests what was the source of his strength. It was Christ who led him among the lepers, and it was Christ who, at this time, was his constant companion. Battles such as he was fighting are not won alone, and Francis was learning more and more to depend upon his Lord. Yet he was still groping in the dark, glad to follow any glimmer of light which showed itself. But the gleams were few and fitful, and he still felt uncertain as to what God wanted him to do. "Return to your own country and you will be told what to do" had been the message which had reached him at Spoleto; but so far he had not been told much. It was a slow business waiting for guidance, and a great test of his faith. Often he would go off to pray in the woods and caves on the side of Mount Subasio where he would remain for several hours waiting upon God and in a perpetual conflict with his lower self. He knew that he had been vain, and now temptation came to him in the fear that if he adopted this new life to which the Spirit seemed to be leading him he would lose all his good looks and his health and perhaps his life. This is revealed in the curious story of how, when in prayer in the woods, he was haunted by the memory of an ugly, old hunch-backed woman from Assisi and the suggestion that, unless he would withdraw from his purpose the devil would transfer the hump to his back.[2] But did health and good looks matter? One thing which Francis was beginning to see was that he must be prepared to give up all the things which he had loved and enjoyed, and that he must go down into the suffering and poverty of the world and take the hump upon his own back. It was no good throwing a coin to a beggar; he must be a beggar himself, dependent upon the charity of his fellow men, as all are dependent upon the charity of God. It was no good "sending a subscription" to the local leper hospital; he must himself go among the lepers as

[1] *Opusc.*, p. 77.   [2] 3 *Soc.* 12.

their equal, and, if need be, become a leper himself. Such were the demands of love.

Not all of this was clear to Francis at first. The first step was to become dissatisfied with his old life. The problem as to what was to take its place, once it was thrown off, was the next thing which this gay adventurer for Christ had to solve.

The third of the "divine visitations" came to him shortly after this in the little ruined church of St Damian, just outside the walls of Assisi. This was one of the places to which Francis was accustomed to go for quiet prayer. Standing alone among the vineyards there was, about it, an air of peace which was soothing to his troubled spirit. The church had fallen very much into decay, and there was a rather decayed old priest living there who still continued to say Mass at its broken-down altar. Behind the altar was a large wooden cross on which was painted the figure of the Crucified in crude, Byzantine style.

It was while praying before this altar that Francis received the third of the visitations of the Lord. He was praying for guidance, for some positive command which would take him forward along the road. At present all seemed uncertain and negative. If only God would give him some clear direction! It was then that the message came. So vivid was it that it seemed as if the figure on the cross was in fact speaking to him, and the words which he heard were these: "Francis, go and repair my church which, as you see, is falling down."[1]

Francis rose to his feet in an ecstasy of joy. Here at last was an answer to his repeated prayers; here was a positive command and a task to which he could immediately set his hand. He looked round at the ruined church—the great holes in the roof, the walls crumbling into decay, the grass and weeds growing up through the floor. How shameful that a "house of God" should be in such a condition while he and his friends lived in their strong, well-built houses! Francis had absolutely no doubt that he was divinely directed to rebuild this tumbled-down church with his own hands.

[1] 3 *Soc.* 13.

The first thing was to find the priest and make arrangements for a light to be kept burning continuously before the altar where Christ had spoken. The next thing was to raise money for the purchase of stones, timber, mortar for the repair of the church, and for this purpose Francis loaded his horse with bales of the richest cloth from his father's shop and rode over to Foligno where he sold the cloth and the horse and walked back to Assisi with a large sum of money in his pocket which he tried to persuade the priest at St Damian's to accept. The priest, however, was a cautious man. Knowing that Francis' father was a hard man, he felt it would be safest to refuse the money in spite of Francis' urgent entreaties, so Francis flung the money, with a gesture of contempt, on to the window-sill.[1]

The priest was right. Francis' father, Peter Bernardone, was in fact extremely angry at what had happened; and, hearing that his son was at St Damian's, he decided to proceed there and bring this nonsense to an end. Then there began a long struggle between father and son which reached its climax when Francis solemnly renounced his sonship before the Bishop of Assisi in the following spring. From the moment of Francis' dejected return from Spoleto his father had realized that the plans which he had made for his son were not likely to be achieved. The strange ideas which Francis seemed to be entertaining were entirely out of keeping with the business instincts of his father, and irritation was bound to ensue. Lavish gifts to the undeserving poor were bad enough, but when it came to associating with lepers and helping himself to cloth out of the family storehouse it was clear to Peter Bernardone that the limit had been reached. It was, therefore, with no love in his heart that he made his angry way to St Damian's to drag his son back and teach him a lesson which he would not quickly forget. But when he got there Francis was not to be found. Full of fear he had crawled into an underground cave where he lay hidden for a whole month. But he could not remain in hiding for ever, and eventually summoned up his courage and presented himself, thin, pale, and ragged, in

[1] 3 *Soc.* 16.

the streets of Assisi, where he began to beg for building material with which to restore the ruined church. When he drew near to his old home, followed by a crowd of boys throwing stones and filth at him, his father suddenly realized that the victim of this rough horseplay was no other than his own son, and, rushing into the street, he dragged him into the house and locked him up in the cellar, where he was later released by his mother. He immediately returned to St Damian's.[1]

In setting about this simple task of rebuilding a ruined church Francis, therefore, had no easy path to follow. The trouble was the way in which he was doing it. If he had set about it in a gentlemanly way, opening a subscription list, soliciting money from his friends, or organizing a garden-party or a ball to raise the money, no one would have raised any objections. But when it came to dressing like a scarecrow and wandering about the streets of Assisi like a common beggar everyone's sense of decency was outraged. No wonder the proud and respectable Peter, with all his social ambitions, was angry. How could he be otherwise?

Terrible though all this was to Francis, he was, at the same time, so completely absorbed by this new life, so certain of his vocation, and so much aware of the divine compulsion that he went about as if in an ecstasy of joy. The chroniclers speak of him at this time as "one drunk with the Spirit", or as if driven forward by "a very intoxication of the divine love".[2] He seemed scarcely to know what he was doing, and was certainly all but unconscious of the buffeting and blows of the mobs which surrounded him and mocked him.

Thus the first effect of the divine message from the cross at St Damian's had been to give Francis something practical to do. After months of doubt and uncertainty his way was now plain. He was to be a builder of ruined churches, an agent for God in the restoration of those portions of his house which the sin and carelessness of man had allowed to fall into decay. But the experience in the little church affected Francis also in

[1] 3 Soc. 17.　　　　　　　　　[2] 3 Soc. 21.

another way. The effect of the previous "stroke" had been to turn his thoughts towards human suffering especially such as concerned the poor and the leprous. Now his thoughts turned more and more towards the sufferings of Christ. It was the suffering Christ who had spoken to him; it was as the servant of the Crucified that he had undertaken this work. Often he had thought, in a casual and impersonal way, of the Passion of Christ, but never before had he felt what that Passion had meant. Now he was overwhelmed with the thought of it, and, for the rest of his life, not only was he liable at any moment to burst into tears when he considered it, but he would also spend many hours in solitary lamentation. Once, we are told, when walking near the church of St Mary of the Angels, he was seen "weeping and wailing with a loud voice. And a devout man hearing him thought he was suffering from some sickness or grief. And, moved by pity toward him, he asked him why he wept. But he said, 'I weep for the Passion of my Lord Jesus Christ, for whom I ought not to be ashamed to go mourning aloud throughout the whole world.' Then that other began likewise to weep with him aloud. And often when Francis rose from prayer, his eyes seemed full of blood, so much and so bitterly was he wont to weep."[1]

We shall never understand St Francis unless we realize the reality and the significance of this deep and bitter sorrow. Over and over again in the legends we find mention of it, for it clearly made a deep impression upon his followers. In a sense Francis never knew quite whether to laugh or cry. He would reprove his disciples for going about with sad and melancholy faces. This was intolerable. The Christian disciple must be radiant with joy, the joy of the redeemed, of the forgiven, of those whom Christ has choosen for his friends. And yet if there was "a time to laugh" there was also "a time to weep". The Christian must be always filled with unspeakable joy when he considers what he might be through the love and mercy of God; but he must also know the unbearable sorrow of considering what he really is and what his sin, and the sins of the

[1] 3 *Soc.* 14.

world, did for his Lord. The thought of the Passion was, therefore, always very near to Francis and sometimes his moments of greatest joy would give place to profound sorrow. One of his disciples described, in later years, how Francis would sometimes be filled with such happiness that he would burst into song, some French romantic song full of life and gaiety and joy. "And sometimes," he went on, "as we have seen with our eyes, he would pick up a stick from the ground, and, putting it over his left arm, would draw across it, as if across a viol, a little bow bent with a string, and, going through the proper motions, would sing in French about the Lord. But often all this ecstasy of joy would end in tears, and the song of gladness would melt into sorrow for the Passion of Christ", and Francis would sit there with the toys in his hands and the tears running down his cheeks.[1]

This intense concentration on the Passion appears to have had its origin in the spiritual experience in St Damian's church when Francis knelt before the crucifix. It turned his thoughts more and more towards the Suffering Servant of God and led to increased bodily austerity and discipline. He reduced his food to a minimum, he spent long hours in prayer, and he began the habit of going from door to door with a beggar's bowl and forcing himself to eat the scraps which he thus collected.

This, naturally, became a matter of general interest in Assisi and goaded Francis' father into further action against his son. He had already tried to deal with the matter himself and had failed completely. He now appealed to the city magistrates to summon Francis before them and force him to restore to his father the goods and money which he had taken away. Francis replied that, being now a servant of the Church, he was not subject to the secular power, and Peter Bernardone was forced to take his complaint to the bishop. Guido, Bishop of Assisi, had watched the developments in Francis' life with much interest and had from time to time been able to give him some advice and help. On the whole he appears as a wise and sympathetic father-in-God, with a real concern for this original

[1] *Spec.* 93.

and unconventional young man and a genuine desire to understand his idiosyncrasies and to help him to fulfil his vocation,
whatever that might be. But when the angry father demanded
a trial the bishop was bound to acquiesce.

Francis was therefore summoned to the bishop's palace and
dutifully obeyed. It was a cold morning in late winter or early
spring, but quite a considerable crowd had assembled to see
how this matter would end. Few can have imagined that
Francis would submit to parental authority, but Peter Bernardone was known to be a proud man who would not like to be
humiliated in public by his own son. So the two stood face to
face while the bishop informed Francis that he must give back
anything which belonged to his father since it was not right
that the Church should benefit from money to which it was
not entitled. At the end of the bishop's speech Francis stepped
forward and, to the consternation of the crowd, stripped off
all his clothes and laid them, with such money as he had, at
the bishop's feet saying: "My lord, I will gladly give back to
him not only the money that belongs to him, but my clothes
also." Then turning to address the crowd he said: "Hear all
ye and understand. Up till now I have called Peter Bernardone my father; but, since I now intend to serve the Lord,
I give back to him the money, about which he was so angry,
and all the clothes which I have had from him, wishing to
say only 'Our Father, which art in heaven' not 'my father,
Peter Bernardone'."[1]

This was as dramatic a moment as Francis could have
wished, and it immediately won for him the sympathy of the
crowd. Yet one must not suppose that Francis, by this startling behaviour, was making a cheap bid for popularity. Far
from it. He had always delighted in the spectacular; and, as
in the past he had dazzled the people of Assisi by his clothes,
now he would dazzle them by his nakedness. The gesture was
dramatic, but it was also symbolic. It marked a complete
break with the past. He had brought nothing into the world
and he was certain that he would carry nothing out. If he had

[1] 3 *Soc.* 19f.

come naked into the world, he would go out of it naked, into a new world, a world where "worldly" standards would mean nothing, a world where love alone reigned. By this sudden action he had irrevocably declared his purpose. There could be no going back.

The next few months were a time of great hardship and loneliness and uncertainty. Francis was committed now to a life of poverty and was immediately faced with the problem which assails all poor people—how to live. The Bishop of Assisi procured the cast-off clothes of one of his outdoor servants to cover Francis' naked body, and thus arrayed he set out on his great adventure into the unknown.

He left Assisi by the northern road and wandered up the valley of the Tescio. But every man's hand seemed to be against him. First a group of robbers set upon him, stripped him of his tunic, flogged him, and threw him into a ditch. When they had gone he managed to crawl to a monastery hoping for food and shelter, but after a day or two's work in the scullery he was turned out again, clad in nothing but a shirt, and so made his way to Gubbio where an old friend of the family provided him with some kind of rough garment. He was indeed learning poverty in a hard school, but his heart remained gay and uplifted as he turned his footsteps back towards Assisi and sought out his old friends at the leper-house. This time he came to them without money and with nothing to give except love and service. But they welcomed him in their misery, and he remained for some time with them attending to their sores and doing what he could to make them comfortable.[1]

Meanwhile the words of the divine message in St Damian's still rang in his ears: "Francis, go and repair my church." There was still work to be done on the old church, and even when that was finished he had no difficulty in finding similar work to do at another church and then at the little chapel of St Mary of the Angels, or of the Little Portion, down in the

[1] *1 Cel.* 16f.

woods. So once again Francis was to be seen in the streets of Assisi begging for stones, begging for oil, begging for his daily bread, all "for the love of God". And so the work went on, and the three little churches began to look more cared for. But of them all the one which he came to love most was the Church of the Little Portion, the Portiuncula, which appealed to him by its simplicity and remoteness and destitution. No one seemed to care much about it, hidden away there in the woods. But to Francis and his friends it became an object of special reverence and devotion, and is now one of the holy places of the world. Francis loved to go there for quiet after the hard work of the day. The very name—the Little Portion —was dear to him, suggestive of poverty and humility; and the fact that it was hidden away and neglected made it an ideal retreat for anyone in search of quiet.

For Francis was still very much in the dark. Looking back over the past year or two, and weighing up his experiences there was not very much to put on the positive side. The story so far had been mainly a story of "giving up". The Spirit had been saying "No"—not knighthood, not Apulia, not popularity, not comfort, not a gay life. And Francis had learnt to submit. One by one the good things of life had been given up. By what Celano calls "the perfect conquest of himself" he had surrendered all the things most dear to him and had allowed himself to be taken down to the very depths, to be the laughing-stock of his fellows, to be thrown into the snow by bandits, and thrown out of a monastery by monks, to make his home among lepers, to suffer cold and hunger, to be without money, without friends, without a home, without security, and without hope of ever living in better circumstances. But all this was negative. On the positive side there was not much to record, little, in fact, except the command to go and repair churches. For some time Francis had been dutifully and willingly obeying this command. But was this the life to which God was calling him? Was it necessary to give up so much just to become an amateur bricklayer and to patch up a few churches which no one really cared much for? So, for Francis there was still much anxiety and uncertainty, and still he prayed for light and leading.

It was on the morning of St Matthias' day, 24 February 1206, that the light broke on him and he reached the end of all his striving and questioning. He was living, at this time, at the Portiuncula, and on that morning he attended Mass in the little chapel. The Gospel for the day told how Christ had sent out his apostles into the world, and as the priest read the well-known words Francis was again visited by God. It does sometimes happen that when we read or hear some quite familiar passage suddenly some phrase seems to stand out from all the rest as if written in letters of gold and solely for our benefit. It is then the Spirit speaks to us with a voice so penetrating and so compelling that it is hard to disobey. It was so with Francis on that morning. Slowly the words were read: "As ye go, preach, saying, The Kingdom of heaven is at hand. Heal the sick, cleanse the lepers, raise the dead, cast out devils: freely ye have received, freely give. Provide neither gold, nor silver, nor brass in your purses, nor scrip for your journey, neither two coats, neither shoes nor yet staves: for the workman is worthy of his meat." To the awe-struck Francis these words were a personal message; they were the answer to all his prayers; and, as the clouds of darkness rolled away, he saw, as clear as day, what Christ was calling him to do.

Once again Christ wished to send out an apostle, and on the same terms as before. Francis was to be that apostle, and all the strange experiences of the last few years had been but a preparation for this moment. He had given up everything, he had gone down to the depths, but now his Lord was raising him up and calling him to his service. As soon as Mass was done Francis cried out in great exultation: "This is what I have been wanting, this is what I have been seeking; this is what I long with all my heart to do." And, in order to make a start on his literal obedience to the Gospel precepts, he tossed aside his staff, kicked off his sandals and, throwing aside his leather belt, he girded himself with a piece of rough cord.[1]

[1] 3 *Soc.* 25.

2

Imitatio Christi

As Francis knotted the rope round his waist on the Feast of St Matthias he probably realized that he was girding himself for a very formidable task. After a gay and opulent youth he had been suddenly checked by a series of divine visitations which had killed all his ambitions and gradually taken from him all the things which he had previously valued and enjoyed. But it was some time before anything very definite had been put in their place. From the time when he had received his first check at Spoleto until the hearing of the Gospel at the Portiuncula he had often been in a mist and darkness so profound as almost to drive him to despair. "Lord, what wilt thou have me do?" had been the question constantly on his lips; and all the vigils and prayers and austerities had failed to secure an answer. The crippling stroke which had checked him in full career on the night of the banquet had directed his thoughts towards poverty, and the message of the Crucified in St Damian's church had given him a task to perform: but it was not until the final visitation at the Portiuncula that the way became at all clear to him. But from that moment he seems to have been in no further doubt. His life was to be nothing less than an "imitation of Christ", conscious, literal, and uncompromising.

There had always been an element of recklessness in Francis' nature. This had contributed to his success as a host and as a "master of the revels". He hated half-measures and calculations, and when he did anything he loved to do it on the grand scale whether it were for his own pleasure or for that of others. Moreover, when the divine visitations began to unsettle his life this quality still persisted. When he suddenly became aware of the self-consciousness of the impecunious knight who was to go with him to Apulia, he did not offer to share his fine equipment with him; he gave him the lot. When he met the leper, he did not satisfy his conscience by merely going up to him and giving him a tip; he embraced him. When he resolved to restore to his father all that he had received from him, he did not merely give back to him the superfluities of life; he stripped himself naked. And when he heard the Gospel read at the Portiuncula he did not resolve just to live a more Christian life; he pledged himself to a literal obedience to every word of Christ.

Here he was soon brought up against great difficulties. No student of the Gospels can have failed to realize that Christ's teaching does contain some very "hard" sayings. Some of these occur in the Sermon on the Mount when Christ is setting out what Christian discipleship involves. After emphasizing blessedness of the poor, the meek, and the persecuted, he goes on to say: "Whosoever shall smite thee on thy right cheek, turn to him the other also. And if any man will sue thee at law and take away thy coat, let him have thy cloak also. . . . Give to him that asketh of thee, and from him that would borrow of thee turn not thou away." And again: "Take no thought for your life, what ye shall eat or what ye shall drink, nor yet for your body, what ye shall put on." This teaching was, presumably, given in the early part of the ministry. As time went on, and the issues became more clearly defined, the demands of Christ became even more severe. In the fourteenth chapter of St Luke's Gospel we see Jesus surrounded by great and admiring crowds, but he suddenly turns and addresses them in words of the utmost austerity: "If any man come to me and hate not his father, and mother, and wife, and children, and brethren, and sisters, yea, and his own life also, he cannot be my disciple. And whosoever doth not bear his cross and come after me, cannot be my disciple. . . . So likewise, whosoever he be of you that forsaketh not all that he hath, he cannot be my disciple." And he concludes with the implication that just as salt which has gone stale is utterly useless, so the disciple who is not prepared to accept these conditions is of no value to the kingdom of God.

Christ is not here speaking of perfection; he is not, apparently, speaking to the inner circle of those who had left all to follow him; he is addressing the crowds about the elementary conditions of discipleship. These appear to be three: hatred of those nearest and dearest to us, the voluntary acceptance of persecution, and the disposal of all our possessions. And these are essential. He is most emphatic about this. Unless a man is prepared to make these sacrifices *"he cannot be my disciple"*. And yet there are hundreds of thousands of men and women who consider themselves Christian disciples who have not the slightest intention of doing any one of these three things.

What can be done about it? We can try, as so many have tried to get round these "hard sayings". We can try to persuade ourselves that Christ never said them, though few can accept so easy an escape as that. We can treat them as "rhetorical exaggerations" which were never meant to be taken seriously; though once we start doing that we can soon water down the teaching of Christ until it loses all its force and originality. We can argue that these conditions were meant only for the innermost circle of the disciples, or that Christ gave them under the (erroneous) belief that the end of the world was imminent; but neither of these explanations can be of much comfort to a troubled conscience. The fact is, that, try as we like, we cannot easily avoid the terrible implication of these "hard sayings" of Christ. We can think them unfair, or absurd, or outrageous, but we cannot deny that they are a statement of what full Christian discipleship involves, or that they lay a very great burden upon our consciences.

It was sayings like these which had troubled the conscience of St Francis and which had caused him so much anxiety, and driven him to such prolonged prayer, until the light dawned upon him and he saw his way quite clearly before him. In one of the ancient prayers of the Church there are two petitions: that we may "perceive and know what things we ought to do" and that we may "have grace and power faithfully to fulfil the same". Many of us are bothered about the first of these, especially in view of the kind of teaching which we have just been considering. But to Francis the first petition soon ceased to have much meaning. If he wanted to know what to do he had only to look at the teaching of Christ and accept that as it stood. The only question was—Would he have "grace and power faithfully to fulfil the same"?

Only on one condition that was that he should become completely indifferent to the consequences of his actions. The trouble about the "hard sayings" is that obedience to them would lead to such dire consequences. The man who seriously tried to order his life according to the teaching of the Sermon on the Mount would have to be prepared to face the possibility of being robbed and cheated, of being often cold and hungry, and perhaps even dying in a ditch within a month. Few, very few, are prepared to take so great a risk. But Francis had counted the cost and was prepared now to take that risk. So great was his faith and so indifferent was he to what might be the outcome of it all, that he was without fear and without anxiety. His only anxiety was that he might fail in his obedience. Apart from that he was unafraid. If he died of exposure within a week it would be God's will that he should do so; and what more glorious than to die in the certainty that you were carrying out the commands of Christ? If he caught leprosy and died a lingering death in a lazar-house, that again would be God's will; and the true Christian must be faithful unto death, whether it be quick or slow. Once faith has overcome all fear of consequences there are no limits to the power of love.

Francis' task now was, first of all, to apply himself most assiduously to assimilate the teaching of Christ so that the way might be plain; secondly, to live always in the closest possible touch with him in order to receive strength and power for what must be a very hard journey; and then to set out quite simply and fearlessly to imitate Christ and to obey his every command. Thus there was inaugurated, at that quiet Mass in

23

the little, forgotten church in the woods, an experiment in Christian living so fascinating and so courageous that it holds the world's admiration to this day.

And yet, to Francis, it was the most natural thing in the world. He claimed no originality, for he was only acting in obedience to teaching which the world had had before it for more than a thousand years. He certainly claimed no special gift of fidelity or sanctity, for, like all true saints, he was fully conscious of his own imperfections. All that he could claim was that, having been told what to do, he had tried to do it, or, as he said at the end of his life: "I have done my duty; may Christ teach you yours."

Once, in the latter part of his life, when things were going badly in the Order, and more and more pressure was being put upon him to allow the friars to break the rule of poverty to the extent of possessing books, St Francis gave a brief summary of his ideals. Brother Leo, his companion and closest friend, tells this in the following way:

> The most holy father was unwilling that his friars should be desirous of knowledge and books, but he willed and preached to them that they should desire to be founded on holy Humility, and to imitate pure Simplicity, holy Prayer, and our Lady Poverty, on which the saints and first friars did build. And this, he used to say, was the only safe way to one's own salvation and the edification of others, since Christ, to whose imitation we are called, showed and taught us this alone by word and example alike.[1]

Here are the four foundation stones of what we may call the "Franciscan Way"—Humility, Simplicity, Poverty, and Prayer—and we shall find that most of the early writings about St Francis, such as the *First Life* by Thomas of Celano and the *Mirror of Perfection*, are largely concerned with these four themes. They are indeed the very essence of what St Francis stood for, and any attempt to understand the ideals for which he strove must begin from this point.

[1] *Spec.* 71.

It is often thought that the most characteristic thing about the friars was their poverty. This was certainly the most obvious feature of their life, but I doubt very much whether St Francis would have regarded it as the most important. Certainly he never placed it first in his teaching. Pride of place was generally given to humility. The friar must ask nothing for himself, and if he asks nothing for himself poverty is bound to follow. So Francis never tired of impressing upon his followers the necessity of humility. The very name which he chose for his fellowship emphasized this point. They were to call themselves "Friars Minor", the "lesser" brothers, the underlings, the scum of the earth, or, as St Paul said: "We are made as the filth of the world, and are the offscouring of all things unto this day." The friars were to make no demands upon society. If men were kind to them they must accept such kindness graciously: if men were rough with them they must take what was given without argument or complaint or retaliation. Poorest of the poor and humblest of the humble they must go their way, happy to be identified with the servile, the outcasts, and the unlovable, glad to be despised and patient in every kind of adversity.

Once when St Francis and Brother Leo were walking from Perugia to St Mary of the Angels in bitterly cold weather, the saint discoursed to his companion upon the subject of "Perfect Joy". There is no passage in any of the early writings about St Francis which more clearly displays the essence of Franciscan humility. As the two men plodded on Francis called thus to Brother Leo:

"Brother Leo, though the Brothers Minor throughout all the world were great examples of sanctity and true edifying, rather write it down and take heed diligently that not therein is perfect joy." And going on a little further, St Francis called a second time: "O Brother Leo, albeit the Brothers Minor should give sight to the blind, make straight the crooked, cast out devils, make the deaf to hear, the lame to walk, the dumb to speak, and (greater still) should raise them that have been dead a four days' space, write that not herein is perfect joy." And going on a little, he cried aloud: "O Brother Leo, if the Brother Minor should know all tongues and all sciences and all scriptures, so that he could prophesy and reveal not only things to come but also the secrets of consciences and souls, write that not therein is perfect joy." . . . And going on a little further, St Francis cried aloud: "O Brother Leo, albeit the Brother Minor could preach so well as to turn all the infidels to the faith of Christ, write, write that not therein is perfect joy." And this manner of speech continuing for full two miles, Brother Leo with much marvel besought him, saying: "Father, I pray thee in the name of God that thou tell me wherein is perfect joy."

And St Francis thus made answer: "When we come to St Mary of the Angels, all soaked as we are with rain and numbed with cold and besmirched with mud and tormented with hunger and knock at the door; and the porter comes in anger and says: 'Who are ye?' and we say: 'We be two of your brethren'; and he says: 'Ye be no true men; nay, ye be two rogues and gad about deceiving the world and robbing the alms of the poor, get ye gone'; and thereat he shuts to the door and makes us stand without in the snow and the rain, cold and a-hungered, till nightfall; if therewithal we patiently endure such wrong and such cruelty and such rebuffs without being disquieted and without murmuring against him; and with humbleness and charity bethink us that this porter knows us full well and that God makes him speak against us; O Brother Leo, write that herein is perfect joy. And if we be instant in knocking and he come out full of wrath and drive us away as importunate knaves, with insults and buffetings, saying: 'Get ye gone hence, vilest of thieves, begone to the alms-house, for here ye shall find nor food nor lodging'; if we suffer this with patience and with gladness and with love, O Brother Leo, write that herein is perfect joy. And if we still constrained by hunger, cold and night, knock yet again and shout and with much weeping pray him for the love of God that he will but open and let us in; and he yet more enraged should say: 'These be importunate knaves, I will pay them well as they deserve', and should rush out with a knotty stick, and, taking us by the hood, throw us upon the ground and send us rolling in the snow, and beat us with all the knots of that stick: if with patience and with gladness we suffer all these things, thinking on the pains of the blessed Christ, the which we ought to suffer for the love of Him: O Brother Leo, write that here and herein is perfect joy.

"Then hear the conclusion of the whole matter, Brother Leo. Above all graces and gifts of the Holy Spirit, that Christ granteth to His beloved, is to overcome oneself, and willingly for the love of Christ endure pains and insults and shame and want: inasmuch as in all other gifts of God we may not glory, since they are not ours but God's; whence saith the Apostle: 'What hast thou that thou hast not received of God? And if thou hast received it of Him, wherefore boastest thou thyself as if thou hadst it of thyself?' But in the cross of tribulation and affliction we may boast, since this is ours; and therefore saith the Apostle: 'I would not that I should glory save in the cross of our Lord Jesus Christ.' "[1]

Here is true humility, the first and most fundamental quality of the Franciscan. "We were simple men and in subjection to all", wrote St Francis of the early days of the Order,[2] and he certainly did his utmost to see that the highest standards of humility were observed. There were two ways in which he drove home this lesson. In the first place he insisted that every newcomer to the fraternity should take his turn in going out begging for food. To many men, especially those who had been rich in the world, this was a severe test of their courage and obedience. But Francis encouraged them, both by word and example, to overcome their shame and to go out boldly,

[1] *Fior.* 8.   [2] *Opusc.*, p. 79.

for, "the nobler my son is," he used to say, "the readier let him be to go, for in suchwise merits are heaping up for him".[1] But if this first test of humility was a hard one, the second test must, to many, have seemed even harder, for this was to go and serve the lepers and live among them. "In the beginning of the Order", writes Brother Leo, "he wished that the friars should abide in leper-houses to serve them, and there lay a foundation of holy humility."[2]

This glorification of humility affected all Francis' thinking, not least in his attitude towards authority, especially the authority of the Church. There were at this time a number of fraternities going about preaching the Gospel and living lives of poverty and simplicity. But they appear not to have had any great interest in humility, which to Francis was essential. Thus whereas these other movements tended to be anti-nomian and anti-clerical Francis insisted that his Order should be directly and wholly under the authority of the Church and that its members should pay special respect to the hierarchy and never set themselves up as rivals of the parochial clergy. "The Lord gave me", he said, "such faith in his priests . . . that even if they should persecute me I wish always to go to them. And even if I had the wisdom of Solomon and should find some poor little priests of this world, I do not wish to preach in their parishes without their consent. And them and all others I wish to fear, to love and to honour as if they were my lords."[3] The friars, therefore, were forbidden to preach unless they had first obtained permission from the priest in charge of the parish, and were taught to treat even the most ignorant and slovenly priest with the utmost respect and honour. It may be that, to some of the friars, this test of humility was even harder than that of going begging or serving the lepers.

Attempts have sometimes been made to suggest that Francis was a rebel against authority and against the Church, but there is no evidence whatever for this assumption. Indeed all the evidence is on the other side. That Francis' shrewd mind was

[1] 2 Cel. 75. [2] Spec. 44. [3] Opusc., p. 78.

sometimes critical of the Church, and that he often suffered much from the failures of the Church and of its ministers, can hardly be doubted. But humility demanded that no censures should be passed and that no privileges should be claimed for those who were trying to show a better way.

Humility is also the key to Francis' attitude towards scholarship, which also became the subject of much controversy, both in his own life and for many years afterwards. Within fifty years of Francis' death the Friars Minor had become the most learned body of men in the world, but this development was entirely opposed to the original wishes of the saint. In spite of many appeals, Francis remained adamant in his refusal to permit the friars to possess books or to allow themselves to get enticed into the academic world. His brethren were called to be neither brilliant preachers nor able controversialists, but simple evangelists preaching their Gospel far more by the quality of their lives than by the eloquence of their words. Many of the leading friars were dismayed at this point of view, but nothing could shake Francis' convictions.

His profound suspicion of learning seems to have arisen from two considerations. In the first place learning was incompatible with absolute poverty. The student must have books and somewhere to read them, whereas the Friar Minor was to be homeless and without possessions of any kind. But if the rule of poverty proved inimical to scholarship even more so did the demand for absolute humility. St Francis was convinced that scholarship led almost inevitably to pride. This was partly due to the scholastic method of disputation in which success tended to be measured by brilliance rather than by knowledge, but it was also due to the fact that learning put one in a position of superiority over one's fellows and made it more difficult for a man to mingle on terms of equality with tramps and lepers, and to regard himself as beneath the contempt of even the most ignorant and depraved of his fellow-men. So St Francis once declared that when a scholar joined the Order he ought, in some way, to give up his learning, just as a rich man gave up his riches, in order that, having stripped himself of such a possession, he might offer himself naked to Christ.

Everything, therefore, which could possibly impair or endanger the profession of absolute humility was to be sternly resisted. But even though a man might humble himself with all his might, and descend to the very depths of human degradation and misery, there still remained the last enemies of humility—self-satisfaction and the applause of men. Francis was as much on guard against complacency as he was against any breach of the rule of poverty. There was something quite disconcerting about his honesty. Once, when he was suffering greatly from his infirmities he had been given some meat-broth to eat. Shortly afterwards, when preaching in Assisi in mid-winter, he suddenly startled his audience by appearing half-naked before them, and with a rope round his neck being dragged along by the respectable Brother Peter Catanii, who was well known in the city. Francis then confessed before the people: "You . . . believe me to be a holy man, but I confess to God and to you that I have eaten in this my infirmity flesh and broth made with flesh."[1] We are told that he had instructed one of the friars to throw ashes in his face, but the friar refused to do it. There was nothing that Francis feared more than to acquire a reputation for sanctity to which he was not really entitled. Few things, therefore, can ever have given him more delight than when a peasant ran up to him and, discovering who he was, said: "Take care to be as good as all men say you are, for there are many who think a lot of you. That's my advice to you; always try and live up to your reputation."[2]

If pride is the deadliest of the seven deadly sins then humility must obviously count for most among the Christian virtues. But though Francis regarded humility as the fundamental quality of life, he would have placed simplicity on a level with it. And, as far as his own life was concerned, simplicity was essential, for his whole way of life was based on the simplest possible interpretation of the Gospels and of the teaching of

[1] *Spec.* 61.   [2] *2 Cel.* 142.

Christ. Most of us tend to make our own terms with Christ; but it was not so with St Francis. For him the most obvious sense of any saying was good enough, so that we find a certain naïvety about his teaching which some might regard as whimsical or even absurd. But it was far from absurd to him: it was a fundamental point in the experiment which he was making. Brother Leo gives us an instance of this. He writes:

At that time when blessed Francis was living with the brethren whom he then had, he lived in such poverty with them, that they observed the Holy Gospel in and through all things to the letter, from that day in which the Lord revealed to him that he and his brethren should live according to the form of the Holy Gospel. Whence he forbade the brother who used to cook for the friars to put dried beans in warm water when they were to be given to the friars to eat on the following day, as the custom is, so that they might observe that saying of the Holy Gospel, *take no thought for the morrow*. And so that brother put off setting them to soften till after Mattins, because by then the day in which they were to be eaten had begun.[1]

To many this may have seemed ridiculous, keeping of the letter rather than the spirit; but to Francis it was quite natural. If you set out to take literally every word of the Gospel, you have no right to dispense yourself from any saying either on the grounds that it is too hard or that it is too small to be of any account.

This is quite typical of St Francis and was part of his simplicity. Another aspect of it was his innocence. Simplicity demanded that the friars should run the risk of being constantly taken in and their confidence abused, as, no doubt, often happened. It also demanded that they should act on impulse rather than on forethought. If a beggar presented himself they must try to satisfy his needs at whatever cost. Once a poor woman came to the Portiuncula begging for alms.

1 *Spec.* 19.

Francis turned to Peter Catanii and asked if they had anything that they could give her. Peter replied that the only thing in the house was the New Testament from which the lessons were read at Mattins. Francis immediately cried: "Give it to her that she may sell it for necessity. For I firmly believe that it will please the Lord and the Blessed Virgin more than if we were to read in it."[1] In the same way nothing could stop Francis from giving away his clothes, even when he was in desperate need of them on account of his illnesses. This caused some embarrassment to those whose responsibility it was to see that the saint was kept warm. Brother Leo tells us:

> At the Celle di Cortona the blessed father was wearing a new mantle which the friars had been at some trouble to obtain for him. A poor man came to the dwelling, weeping for his dead wife and his poor, orphaned family, to whom the saint, full of compassion, said, "I give you this mantle on condition that you will not give it up to anyone except he buy it from you and pay you well." The friars, hearing this, ran together to the poor man to take away that mantle from him. But the poor man, gathering boldness from the face of the holy father, with clutching hands was carrying it away as his own. At last the friars redeemed the mantle, promising that the correct price should be given to the poor man.

And he adds:

> We who were with him bear testimony of him that he was of so much charity and pity for the sick and the whole, not only toward his brethren but also toward other poor folk, well or ill, that he used to give to the poor those necessaries of his body which the brethren used sometimes to acquire with great solicitude and labour, first soothing us lest we should be troubled by it, with great joy, inward and outward, taking away from himself even those things which were very necessary to him. Wherefore the Minister

[1] *Spec.* 38.

General and his Guardian had ordered him not to give his tunic to any friars without their leave.[1]

There is here great simplicity. None of those distinctions were drawn between the "deserving" and the "undeserving" poor. To the Friar Minor it should be a disgrace to find anyone poorer than himself, and therefore every poor man was an object of compassion whatever the cause of his poverty might be. Simplicity also demanded that the friars should seek no privileges for themselves, and that the Order as a whole should be content to do its work according to the opportunities which God gave and without asking for special consideration. "I strictly command all the brethren on obedience," wrote St Francis in his will, "that, wherever they may be, they shall not dare to ask for any letter from the Roman court, neither by themselves nor by some intermediate person, neither for a church nor for any other place, neither for purposes of preaching nor because of any persecution of their bodies; but, if in any place they are not received, let them flee to some other place where they may do penance with the blessing of God."[2]

The third foundation stone of the Franciscan building was holy poverty. Francis had been brought up in materialistic surroundings and knew the evils which lurk there. He had discovered also that there could be plenty of materialism in the Church as well as in secular society. He had seen the scramble for money and the power which money can bring. And he had renounced it all. By humility he had renounced the power; by poverty he renounced the money.

To the average man poverty is a negative. The poor are the "have-nots", and a man becomes poor by losing his money or his property. But it was not so regarded by St Francis. To him poverty was an ideal and a personality. It became the Lady Poverty, to be wooed and won like any other bride. Poverty was the handmaid of Christ, who alone remained faithful to him and who alone mounted the cross with him. "Alone thou

<hr>

[1] *Spec.* 31.   [2] *Opusc.*, p. 80.

33

didst cleave to the King of Glory," says the author of that delightful allegory the *Sacrum Commercium*,

> when all the chosen and beloved of Him fearfully deserted Him. But thou, most faithful bride, most sweet lover, never for a moment didst leave His side—nay, then to Him thou didst the more cleave, the more thou didst see Him despised of all. . . . Thou was with Him in the revilings of the Jews, in the mockings of the Pharisees, in the cursings of the Chief Priest, in the buffeting, the spitting, the scourging. He whom all should have revered was mocked by all, and thou alone didst bear Him company. Nor didst thou leave Him in the hour of death, the death of the Cross, and on the Cross itself, when His body was bared, His arms stretched out, His hands and His feet pierced, with Him thou didst suffer.[1]

These words were not written until several years after the death of St Francis, but they perfectly represent his feelings about poverty. In his romantic way he gallantly took up the cause of the Lady Poverty and became her servant and her champion. And just because she was regarded as the enemy of mankind, so Francis, in his topsy-turvy way, treated her as the most holy and lovable of companions. Nothing was too great a sacrifice in her honour, and Francis was constantly devising new ways of serving her. Like every true knight he would allow no word to be said against her, and was quick to jump to her defence. While others sought wealth and despised poverty, Francis sought poverty and despised wealth; and the more poverty was feared so much the more he clung to her side. No wonder he could say in his Testament, "the things which had seemed bitter to me were turned into sweetness of soul and body".[2]

Francis had lived among men who were anxious to get rich. He knew the price they were prepared to pay and the sacrifices which they were ready to make in the pursuit of their ambition. He had seen his father leave the comforts and security

---

[1] *Sac. Com.*, p. 47. [2] *Opusc.*, p. 77.

of his home to make long and dangerous journeys over the Alps and into France in search of rich fabrics which would bring in money, and he knew that fortunes are not easily made and that man who wishes to succeed must devote his whole care and attention to his work. So it was with his own pursuit of poverty, which was just as elusive as wealth. Francis knew well enough that the search for poverty would also involve much sacrifice and labour and demand all his attention. He therefore set himself to seek absolute poverty with all his heart and to resist every attempt to waylay him or to persuade him to be satisfied with any half-measures.

The rule that the friars might on no account accept any money meant that in the early days they were often destitute and so hungry that they almost perished. Several stories of the early years of friars crying out with hunger; but no relaxation of the rule was permitted. Often too they were desperately cold, for Francis would allow only the very minimum of clothing, just the single tunic with cord and breeches. To many of the friars this was hopelessly inadequate during the winter months, and even Francis himself sometimes felt the cold to be almost unendurable. An English friar records how Francis was once nearly overcome with the cold, but instead of succumbing, he boldly took off the single habit which he was wearing and exposed his naked body to the sharp wind in order that he might then thank God that he had at least one garment to cover him.[1] Hard though it was to stand up to such privations, yet the friars knew that it was the reward of serving so exacting a lady as the Lady Poverty, and they rejoiced.

Moreover since Francis had pledged himself and his brotherhood to the pursuit of poverty he was always particularly grieved with those who were false to their profession, even in the smallest details. Once he had made himself a little hut where he could retire for prayer and would spend many hours there.

[1] *A New Fior.*, p. 42.

But one day, when he had gone out of that cell, a certain friar went to see it, and afterward came to the place where the blessed Francis was. And when the blessed father saw him he said to him: "Where do you come from, brother?" And he said: "I have been to your cell." And the blessed Francis said: "Because you have called it mine, another must use it in future, for I shall not go there again." Then he added: "The Lord when He remained in the open air and fasted forty days and forty nights did not cause a cell or a house to be made for Him there, but lay under the rocks of the mountain."[1]

The whole incident is typical of the saint. In the first place he insists that if there is to be any building at all it must be of the very humblest, just a rough hut made of a few branches. But even with that Francis' conscience seems to be troubled; for when it is inadvertently spoken of as his, he immediately refuses to have anything more to do with it. And then his mind flies back to Christ on the mountainside, and he realizes that the imitator of Christ ought not to allow himself even the simplest kind of covering.

Thus was poverty served; but not without great difficulty and constant vigilance. There were so many ways in which her followers might be led astray through thoughtlessness or carelessness. But there was one danger of which Francis was fully conscious and against which precautions could be taken and that was money. Money, to St Francis, was just filth. If you found any filth in your house you naturally got rid of it without delay, and the friar must do the same if he found any money. "Let dung and money," he said, "be loved and valued alike."[2] Not only were the friars strictly forbidden to receive any money, but they were taught that they must not touch it on any account. Celano tells the following story of a friar who carelessly broke this rule.

One day a certain layman came to the church of St Mary of the Portiuncula to pray, and placed some money near the

[1] *Spec.* 9.   [2] 2 *Cel.* 65.

cross as an offering. When he withdrew one of the brothers simply touched it with his hand and threw it on the window-sill. The saint heard of what the brother had done; and the brother, seeing that he was found out, ran to beg for pardon, and, falling on the ground, offered to submit to stripes. The saint rebuked him, and after chiding him most severely for having touched the money, bade him remove it in his mouth from the window-sill, and with his mouth lay it on asses' dung outside the precincts. And while that brother gladly obeyed this command the hearts of all that heard of it were filled with fear.[1]

If poverty was the enemy of wealth, then money must equally be the enemy of poverty, and Francis was perfectly logical in treating it as the accursed thing.

Poverty, therefore, was to be absolute; the friar was to call nothing his own, not even the shabby clothes in which he stood. Yet, it must not be supposed that poverty was an end in itself. The achievement of an almost unendurable poverty was to be the aim of the Franciscan, but only because poverty was the gateway to spiritual freedom. "How hardly shall they that have riches enter into the Kingdom of God", said the Lord; and though Francis would have been the first to admit that there were great saints to be found among the rich and great sinners among the poor, yet he would have maintained that it really was very much easier to be a faithful disciple if you were poor than if you were rich.

About the year 1211 Francis and Brother Masseo set off on a journey to France. Having reached a small town, suffering much from hunger, each went to beg for food. Masseo being tall and handsome did well; but Francis being small and insignificant got nothing but a few scraps of dry bread. When they met again by a fountain Francis exclaimed: "O Brother Masseo, we are not worthy of such vast treasure." But Masseo protested that this was really absurd when they had so little to eat and no place of their own in which to eat it. But Francis

[1] 2 Cel. 65.

was quite impenitent. "This it is", he cried, "that I account vast treasure, wherein is nothing at all prepared by human hands but whatsoever we have is given by God's own providence, as manifestly doth appear in the bread that we have begged, in the table of stone so fine, and in the fount so clear; wherefore I will that we pray unto God that He make us to love with all our heart the treasure of Holy Poverty which is so noble that thereunto did God Himself become a servitor."

Then, a little later, he added these words:

Dearest friend, let us go to Saint Peter and Saint Paul and pray them to teach us and help us to possess the immeasurable treasure of most Holy Poverty; for it is a treasure so high excelling and so divine that we be not worthy to lay it up in our vile vessels; since this is that celestial virtue whereby all earthly things and fleeting are trodden under foot, and whereby all hindrances are lifted from the soul, so that freely she may join herself to God eternal. And this is the virtue that makes the soul, still tied to earth, hold converse with the angels in heaven, and this it is which hung with Christ upon the cross, with Christ was buried, with Christ rose again, with Christ ascended into heaven; the which also in this life grants to the souls that love it an easier flight to heaven; in that it guards the arms of true humility and love. Wherefore let us pray the most holy apostles of Christ, the which were perfect lovers of this Gospel pearl, that they may beg for us this grace from our Lord Jesus Christ, that of His most holy mercy He may make us worthy to become true lovers, followers, and humble disciples of the most precious, most lovable and gospel poverty.[1]

This passage exactly expresses the views of St Francis. The purpose of poverty is to free the soul from every earthly hindrance that it may be joined to God, and to substitute for the riches of this world the riches of heaven. Like St Paul the friar could describe himself "as poor yet making many

[1] *Fior.* 13.

rich, as having nothing and yet possessing all things". Or, as
the Franciscan poet, Jacopone da Todi, put it:

> Povertate è nulla havere,
> e nulla cosa poi volere;
> ed omne cosa possedere
> en spirito de libertate.

> Poverty is naught to have, and nothing to desire;
> and all things to possess in the spirit of liberty.[1]

Poverty, together with humility and simplicity, opened the
gate to that "closer walk with God" which is the chief end of
man. We shall misunderstand the spirit of St Francis completely if, for one moment, we forget that his whole desire was
to please God and to live in the closest touch with him. Books
have been written on Francis as the inaugurator of what is
called "the Social Gospel"; and it is, of course, true that he
did arouse the consciences of men to the miseries of the poor
and the lepers. But the mainspring of his life was not compassion for his fellow men but an intense love of God from
which naturally flowed not only love for man but for all
creatures. All that St Francis accepted, and bore, and suffered
was in obedience to what he knew to be the will of God.

Francis' own mystic life is revealed in many passages in the
early legends, but there is probably nothing more characteristic
than the story of the night which he spent in the house of
Bernard of Quintavalle about the year 1209. Francis, still
ploughing a lonely furrow in his privations and his church
building, had been invited to spend a night in the house of this
rich citizen of Assisi. The two men slept in one room, and
soon after they had retired to bed Francis rose silently and
began to pray. Only four words escaped his lips—"*Deus
meus et omnia*" ("My God and my all")—but he continued
to murmur these words over and over again until daybreak.
Such an example shows us something of the greatness and
depth of Francis' spiritual insight, his sense of divine majesty

[1] E. Underhill, *Jacopone da Todi*, p. 167.

and of human insignificance. In these simple words lies a whole range of religious experience. Even in those early days Francis was wholly absorbed in God and needed nothing else than to contemplate the mystery of divine transcendence.

Such love towards God, and such dependence upon him was something which St Francis bore with him all through his life. He could never pass a church without going into it to pray, and even the chance arrangement of a couple of twigs in a hedge would remind him of the cross and drive him to his knees in "wonder, love, and praise". The early writers speak of his feeling himself "suddenly visited by the Lord", or of his "gradually becoming aware of the touch of grace", and it appears that these moments of ecstasy came upon him quite unexpectedly and quite irresistibly. At such times he was driven to pray whatever the conditions might be; but, to avoid publicity, he would "make a little cell of his cloak" or "cover his face with his sleeve". While the ecstasy lasted Francis, like other great mystics, became entirely unaware of what was going on around him. Once, says Celano:

> he was riding on an ass at a time when he must needs pass through Borgo San Sepolcro, and as he intended to rest at a certain leper's house, it became known to many that the man of God was to pass by. Men and women flocked from all sides to see him, desiring with their wonted devotion to touch him. What then? They handled him, they pulled him along and cut off little bits from his tunic to put away. He seemed insensible to it all, and heeded what was going on as little as a corpse. At length he and his company reached their destination, and, having long since left Borgo San Sepolcro, the contemplator of heavenly things (as though coming back from elsewhere) anxiously enquired when they would be getting near Borgo?[1]

Though Francis loved to pray in a church and though he had a very special devotion towards the Sacrament, I think it remains true that his greatest moments of prayer were when

[1] 2 Cel. 95.

he was alone in a wood or on a mountain-top. Often he would steal away from his companions and retire to some lonely spot where he could be entirely alone with God. So rapt did he then become that he would often remain all night in prayer. Celano writes:

> He used often to choose out solitary places in order that he might therein wholly direct his mind to God. . . . For his safest haven was prayer: not prayer for one moment, not vacant or presumptuous prayer, but long-continued, full of devotion, calm and humble; if he began late he scarce ended with morning. Walking, sitting, eating, and drinking, he was intent on prayer. He would often go alone by night to pray in churches which were deserted, or in lonely places, wherein, under the protection of God's grace, he got the better of many fears and distresses of mind.[1]

Humility, simplicity, poverty, and prayer were the four foundation stones of the Franciscan way, and the effect of them on the life of the saint was to condemn him to a life of perpetual hardship and suffering. Yet it was in this hardship and suffering that he found the secret of happiness. "Write, Brother Leo, that here and herein is perfect joy."

But to the ordinary man—even the ordinary Christian—the way seems so hard as to be almost grotesque, for Francis despised all those things which the world holds dear. If asked what was most worth having in life many people would say "Health". But to Francis health was of no consideration at all. From the moment when he kissed the leper's hand to the end of his life he was constantly exposing himself to every kind of infection and danger. His bodily austerity, his open-air life in all kinds of weather, his mingling with the poor and the diseased, all combined to weaken and assault his body, and with the inevitable result that for years he was never out of pain and in the last part of his life—blind, diseased, emaciated —it was a wonder that the spirit could survive in a body so broken. Yet, to Francis, all this was joy unspeakable for it

[1] 1 *Cel.* 71.

41

brought him nearer to Christ, the Suffering Servant of God.

If he totally despised the care of the body so also did he despise the ordinary things which men crave. He loathed prosperity and chose poverty for his ideal; he hated security and gave no thought for the morrow; he shunned the approbation of men knowing it to be a source of spiritual pride. His whole life, therefore, was a living contradiction of the way of the world, his aim the very opposite of what most men try to attain.

At Thessalonika the early Christians were described as the men who had "turned the world upside down". Whatever was meant by this phrase, it would certainly apply to St Francis, for he reversed all the usual values and lived in what might almost be called a "looking-glass" world in which the things most to be desired were things like poverty and contempt, cold and hunger, suffering and death. Well might one say that Francis "turned the world and its standards upside down". But which is the right way up?

To the average man the way of St Francis must seem outrageous, fantastic, absurd. And yet is it not the way of Christ? Everything that Francis did was based upon the teaching of Christ. He made no claim to originality: he was only trying to do what the Gospels told him to do. For his one and only wish was to follow Christ, literally, faithfully, and without fear. And if that was his aim, can anyone say that he could have done otherwise?

Many years after Francis' death one of his followers, Pier Pettignano, had a vision. "He saw in vision a superb procession of Apostles, Saints and Martyrs, with the Blessed Virgin at their head, all walking carefully and scrutinizing the ground with much earnestness, that they might tread as nearly as possible in the very footsteps of Christ. At the end of this pageant of the Church Triumphant came the little shabby figure of Francis, barefoot and brown-robed; and he alone was walking easily and steadily in the actual footprints of our Lord."

3
Expansion

FOR the first year or two after his conversion Francis was ploughing a very lonely furrow. Up to the time when he heard the crucifix speak to him in St Damian's he had led a very sociable life. But from the moment when he began his church building he had abandoned his old social life and had adopted a new, strange life of poverty and mendicancy which almost completely cut him off from both his family and his friends. His mother did what she could for him, but his father was obviously the ruling force in the household, and from the day of his journey to Foligno until his death there is no record of Francis having ever crossed the threshold of his own home, except when he was dragged in by his father to be locked up in the cellar. His brothers seem to have been mildly contemptuous of the whole affair, and probably secretly resented the notoriety which his outrageous conduct had brought upon the family. His friends dropped him now that he could not join in their revels and pay their bills. Only two people showed him any sympathy at this time. One was the Bishop of Assisi who did his best to understand this wayward child of God, and the other was the priest at St Damian's who would probably have been of more help to him if he had not been so mortally scared of Francis' father. One other friend is mentioned in the records, the companion who went with Francis on his expeditions to the woods for prayer and meditation, but he seems to have played an entirely passive part, so much so that neither his name nor any remark of his has been preserved. No one really understood what Francis was trying to do, and it was some time before anyone showed any signs of wanting to share in it.

These two or three years of loneliness were a great trial to so sociable a man as St Francis. This loss of friendship and companionship was part of the price which he had to pay in obedience to the divine call, and no doubt he had counted the cost. But it must, all the same, have made those years a period of great hardship. And yet, what could one expect? Francis was quite convinced that God had revealed to him a certain way of life which he must follow at whatever cost. But there was no reason to suppose that God would call anyone else by the same way. So Francis plodded on with his building and his begging, a very lonely figure in the streets of Assisi and in the woods and fields of the surrounding country. Few spoke to him except in mockery; his only friends now were the lepers and one or two village priests.

But a life of such goodness and obedience could hardly be ignored; and, while Francis went his way, more eyes were following him in love and admiration than he imagined. Among those who watched his movements was a rich man of Assisi, Bernard of Quintavalle, older than Francis and a man of considerable standing in the city. There still stands in Assisi his fine *palazzo* within whose walls a strange event took place which marked the end of Francis' years of loneliness, and profoundly affected the whole of his life.

Bernard had watched Francis' life very closely in the last few years, and he was enormously impressed by his church building and by his austerity; but he was still a little doubtful how far it was genuine. Was all this being done really for the love of God, or was it in the nature of a "stunt"? Was Francis really overwhelmed with love towards God, or was there, in his strange behaviour, an element of self-love, or pride, or display? Bernard decided to put this to the test and invited Francis to spend a night with him in his palace.

The story of what happened during that night can best be told in the delightful language of the *Fioretti*. Having prepared a bed for his guest in his own room the two men retired for the night

44

and thereat Bernard set it in his heart to watch his sanctity: wherefore he let make ready for him a bed in his own proper chamber in which at night-time ever a lamp did burn. And Saint Francis, for to hide his sanctity, when he was come into the chamber, incontinent did throw himself upon the bed and made as though he slept: and likewise Bernard after some short space set himself to lie down and fell snoring loudly, in fashion as though he slept right soundly. Whereby Saint Francis, thinking truly that Bernard was asleep, in his sleep rose up from his bed and set himself to pray, lifting up his hands and eyes unto heaven, and with exceeding great devotion and fervour said: "My God and my all!" And thus saying and sorely weeping he abode till morning, always repeating "My God and my all!" and naught beside; and this Saint Francis said while musing on and marvelling at the excellence of the divine Majesty, which deigned to stoop down to a perishing world and through His poor little Francis purposed to bring a remedy for the salvation of his soul and souls of others. Therefore, illumined by the Holy Spirit, or the spirit of prophecy, foreseeing what great things this God would do through him and his Order, and minding him of his own insufficiency and little worth, he cried unto God and besought Him that by His pity and almighty power, without the which the weakness of man may naught avail, He would supply his lack, aid and fulfil what was nothing worth. Bernard seeing, by the light of the lamp, the most devout acts of Saint Francis, and devoutly pondering the words that he spake, was touched and inspired by the Holy Spirit to change his life; in the morning therefore he called Saint Francis and thus bespake him: "Brother Francis, I am wholly purposed in my heart to leave the world and follow thee in whatsoever thou mayest bid me."[1]

Francis was obviously somewhat taken aback by this. The life which he had chosen was so hard that few could endure it, especially a man of Bernard's age and standing. Francis

[1] *Fior.* 2.

was therefore reluctant to accept him until he had satisfied himself beyond all doubt that this offer was prompted solely by the Holy Spirit. The two went, therefore to the bishop's house where they heard Mass and remained praying until Terce. Then Francis invited the priest to open the Gospel-book at random. On the first opening the text which caught his eye was: "If thou wilt be perfect, go and sell that thou hast and give to the poor, and follow me." The second opening revealed the words: "Take nothing for your journey", and the third: "If any man will come after me, let him deny himself and take up his cross and follow me." This put the matter beyond any doubt; Bernard sold all his possessions, distributed the proceeds to the poor, put on the shabby clothes of a mendicant, and joined the saint in his church building. What this meant to St Francis can hardly be imagined. The years of loneliness were now over. Francis had been vindicated in his strange career. The fellowship which came to be called "the Penitents of Assisi" had begun.

Francis' first disciple was not, as might have been expected, some young fire-brand, but a middle-aged City Councillor. His second was Peter Catanii to be followed shortly afterwards by a priest whose first appearance in our story was by no means happy one. While Bernard was distributing money to the poor in the streets of Assisi a certain priest called Silvester happened to pass by, and seeing so much money being given away, remembered that he had sold stones to Francis for his building and had not asked as high a price as he might have done. Now was his chance to make up the deficit. So he complained that he had been underpaid, and Francis, with complete recklessness, showered gold upon him, far more than he was entitled to. Silvester went off in triumph: but it was not long before his conscience began to trouble him. It is annoying to be underpaid for anything, but humiliating to be overpaid; and Silvester began to feel uncomfortable. Within a short time he was back again, asking for pardon and pleading to be received into the fellowship. That made four. The next to join the community was the mystic Giles, so humble that he was always going out of his way to do menial tasks for the poor, and so ecstatic that the children of Perugia used to shout out "Paradise, Paradise" when he passed by in order to see him go into a trance. Then came two others of whom very little is known, and so the community grew.

When there were seven of them Francis decided that the time had come for them to begin some kind of active evangelistic work. So far Francis had remained in or near Assisi since his conversion, and had been mainly occupied in restoring ruined churches. But now that God had sent him a band of helpers it was time to think out how they could best serve him. Possibly Francis at this time began to see more clearly what the Crucified had really meant when he charged him to go and repair his church which was falling down. At first it had seemed obvious enough. Here was a church falling down; he would immediately start to repair it. And for nearly three years Francis had been content with this very simple interpretation. But now that they had become a brotherhood of penitents was it possible that Christ was calling them to something more than just masons' work, and that they were in some way to strengthen the whole Church of God through their lives and through their preaching.

Francis was surrounded by problems. Quite suddenly this little community had come into being, putting new responsibilities on to his shoulders and new questions into his mind. In his uncertainty he again sought the advice of Guido, the Bishop of Assisi. But all that the bishop could do was to suggest that perhaps the standards which they had set themselves were too high and the rule of absolute poverty too hard. To this Francis replied with some spirit: "My Lord, if we should have possessions we should need arms to protect ourselves. For thence arise disputes, and law-suits, and for this cause the love of God and of our neighbour is wont oft-times to be hindered, wherefore we be minded to possess naught of this world's goods."[1] The bishop was speechless in face of such convictions, and Francis went back to his brethren.

[1] 3 Soc. 35.

By this time he had decided that they should divide into small parties and go out to preach repentance and obedience to the commandments of God. He knew that they would have to face much hardship and misunderstanding, that they would be insulted and mocked and ill-treated, and that they would run the risk of dying of starvation, but all this would be a test of their sincerity. Thus the first missionary journeys were undertaken, Francis taking Giles as his companion and going to Ancona.

All that Francis had predicted came true, for the friars had to endure much persecution. "Some heard them gladly," say the early chroniclers,

> others in contrary wise mocked them . . . many thought them deceivers or deceived, nor were minded to receive them into their houses, lest they might prove to be thieves who would carry off their goods by stealth. Wherefore in many places after injury had been done unto them they would shelter in the porches of churches or of houses. For, as hath been said, when both small and great did revile and injure them, they would at times tear from them even the very beggarly garments they had. Then when the servants of God were left naked, for that according unto the precept of the Gospel they wore one tunic only, they would not petition for that which had been seized to be restored unto them. If indeed any, moved by pity, were minded to restore that which had been seized, they received it back gladly. Some would place dice in their hands, and ask if they were minded to play. Others taking hold of their hoods from behind would carry them on their backs as though hanged by an halter. These and suchlike outrages did they unto them, thinking them so despicable that they did boldly torment them as they would. Manifold, moreover, were the tribulations they endured, and narrow were the straits wherethrough they did pass by reason of hunger and thirst and cold and nakedness. Nevertheless these they bore with constancy and patience as they had been exhorted by the

Blessed Francis, nor were they thereby cast down with sadness, nor did they speak evil unto them that did evil entreat them.[1]

When they had returned to Assisi and were resting for a while at the Portiuncula five more men came to join them and so the number of the friars rose to the apostolic figure of twelve. Francis was puzzled by this steady growth and went off into the woods to pray. Things, he felt, were being taken out of his hands. He had begun as a solitary, a hermit, a restorer of churches, content in the belief that he was acting in accordance with the will of God. Then Bernard had joined him and there could be no doubt that he was sent by God. And so with the others. But where was this to end? Was this little fellowship destined to grow into a great Order? Francis shrank from such a development and from the responsibilities which it would bring. He had not bargained for this when he answered the call of the Crucified at St Damian's.

So he went into the woods to pray, and there, while in a kind of trance, he saw a vision of men coming from all over Europe to swell the numbers of the friars. Celano tells us that "he was caught up with himself, and wholly absorbed in a certain light; the capacity of his mind was enlarged, and he beheld clearly what was to come to pass". And he adds that when he returned to his brethren "he seemed changed into another man".[2] The fears, the hesitations, the reluctance had gone, and Francis looked forward fearlessly into the future. "I have seen", he said, "a great multitude of men coming to us, and desiring to live with us in the habit of holy life and under the rule of Blessed Religion. And lo! there is still in mine ears the sound of them as they go and return at the bidding of holy obedience. I have seen as it were the ways filled with the multitude of them assembling in these parts out of almost every nation. Frenchmen are coming, Spaniards hastening, Germans and English running, and a mighty multitude of diverse other tongues are speeding."[3]

[1] 3 *Soc.* 37ff.   [2] 1 *Cel.* 62.   [3] 1 *Cel.* 27.

But this raised new problems. The simple friendship and communal life could not go on much longer. These vast numbers would make some kind of organization necessary. The little fellowship of penitents was to become a great religious Order, and no religious Order can exist without a Rule. But Francis did not care much for rules. They had their rule —the teaching and example of Christ in the Gospels. What more did they want? Yet Francis knew in his heart that this was not enough. In spite of all the dangers which a Rule would introduce—dangers of complacency, of Pharisaism, of disputes over interpretation—he knew that his Order could never be formally recognized unless they could state what it was that they stood for. There were plenty of religious fraternities going about and embarrassing the Church, and Francis did not want his Order just to be classed as one of them. Above all things he wanted to be loyal to the Church and to receive papal sanction and blessing. But he knew well enough that if he ever came face to face with that shrewd old man, Innocent III, he would have to have some document in which was clearly set forth the ideals which this band of men were trying to achieve.

So Francis set himself to write a Rule. As he tells us himself in his Testament, this first Rule was very short and simple. It consisted really of little more than a few texts from the Gospels with a word or two of explanation added. Unfortunately the scroll on which this way of life was set forth has long been lost, but it is not difficult to reconstruct it from other documents. It is of such importance in understanding the early history of the Franciscan Order that it is worth quoting in full in what appears to have been something like its original form.

IN THE NAME OF THE FATHER, AND OF THE SON
AND OF THE HOLY GHOST.   AMEN.

Brother Francis shall promise obedience and reverence to the Lord Pope Innocent and his successors.

1. The Rule and Life of the Brothers is this: to live in obedience, in chastity and without property, and to follow the teaching and footsteps of Christ, who says: *If thou wilt be perfect, go and sell that thou hast and give to the poor and thou shalt have treasure in heaven, and come follow me*; and: *If any man will come after me let him deny himself and take up his cross and follow me*; and again: *If any man come to me and hate not his father and mother and wife and children and brothers and sisters, yea, and his own life also, he cannot be my disciple*; and: *Everyone that hath forsaken father or mother or brothers or sisters or wife or children or houses or lands for my sake shall receive a hundredfold, and shall inherit eternal life.*

2. If any man, by divine inspiration and willing to accept this life, shall come to the brothers, let him be kindly received by them; and he must sell all his goods and be careful to give everything to the poor. And let all the brothers be dressed in shabby clothes, and let them patch them with sackcloth or other rags with the blessing of God; for our Lord says: *They which are gorgeously apparelled and live delicately are in King's houses.* And they may eat anything that is set before them according to the Gospel: *Eat what is set before you.*

3. None of the brethren shall have any power or domination, especially among themselves. As our Lord says in the Gospel: *The princes of the Gentiles exercise dominion over them, and they that are great exercise authority over them,* but it shall not be so among the friars: but *whosoever would be the greatest among them let him be their minister* and servant; and *he that is the greatest among them let him be as the younger.* And no one is to be called prior, but all alike shall be called Friars Minor. And let each wash one another's feet.

4. All the brothers, in whatever place they may be staying with other people, to serve them and work for them, shall not be chamberlains or chancellors nor have any rule over the households of those whom they serve; nor shall they take any office which might cause scandal or harm to the

soul; but let them be underlings and in subjection to all who are in that house. And those brothers who know how to work shall work and pursue whatever trade they have learnt, so long as it is not contrary to the good of the soul and can be honestly carried on. And for their labour they may receive all things necessary, but not money. And when necessary let them go begging like the other brethren.

5. All the brothers must seek to follow the humility and poverty of our Lord Jesus Christ, and must remember that we ought not to possess anything in this world except what the Apostle says: *Having food and raiment let us be therewith content.* And they ought to rejoice when they are living among common and despised people, among the poor and the weak, the sick and the lepers, and those who beg by the wayside. And when it is necessary, let them go for alms and not be ashamed.

6. All the brothers must be careful not to speak evil of one another nor to wrangle; but rather they should make a point of being silent whensoever God shall confer His grace upon them. Nor must they quarrel among themselves nor with others, but must take care to answer humbly, saying: *We are unprofitable servants.* And let them love one another, as our Lord says: *This is my commandment; that ye love one another as I have loved you.*

7. When the brothers are going about the world they must carry nothing with them, *neither scrip, nor bread, nor money, nor staff.* And *into whatsoever house they shall enter, they shall first say:* "Peace be to this house." *And in the same house they shall remain eating and drinking such things as they give.* They shall *not resist evil,* but *unto him that smiteth them upon the cheek let them offer also the other, and him that taketh away their cloak let them not forbid to take their coat also.* Let them *give to every man that asketh of them,* and *of him that taketh away their goods* let them *ask them not again.*

8. Let all the brothers, wherever they may be, remember that they have given themselves and surrendered their bodies

52

to our Lord Jesus Christ for love of whom they ought to expose themselves to their enemies both visible and invisible. As our Lord says: *Whosoever shall lose his life for my sake, the same shall find it unto eternal life.*

9. All the brothers shall be catholics and live and speak as catholics. If, however, any shall err from the catholic faith and life, either by word or deed, and shall not mend his way let him be expelled from our Brotherhood. And let us treat all clerks and religious as our superiors in everything that concerns the salvation of the soul and is not contrary to our religion, and let us respect their order and their office and work in the Lord.

10. And this or some such exhortation and praise shall all my brothers proclaim wherever they like, and among whomsoever they may be, with the blessing of God: "Fear and honour, praise and bless, give thanks and adore the Lord God Almighty, Three in One, Father, Son and Holy Spirit, Maker of all things. *Repent ye and bring forth fruits worthy of repentance*, knowing that we shall shortly die. *Give and it shall be given unto you. Forgive and ye shall be forgiven, And if ye do not forgive men their trespasses neither will the Lord forgive you your trespasses. Confess all your sins.* Blessed are they who die in penitence for they shall be in the Kingdom of God. Woe to those who die not in penitence for they shall be children of the devil whose works they do, and they shall go into the eternal fire. Beware and keep yourselves from all evil, and persevere unto the end in what is good."

In the name of the Lord I beseech all the brothers to learn the purpose and meaning of those things that are written in this way of life, to the salvation of our souls, and to commit them frequently to memory. And I pray God the Almighty, Three in One, that He may bless all those who teach or learn or hold or memorize or do these things, whensoever they call to mind and carry out the things which are written here for our salvation. And I implore them all, kissing their feet, to respect, keep and lay up all these things.

GLORY BE TO THE FATHER, AND TO THE SON,
AND TO THE HOLY GHOST. AS IT WAS IN THE
BEGINNING, IS NOW, AND EVER SHALL BE;
WORLD WITHOUT END.

AMEN.[1]

With this precious document in his bosom Francis and his eleven disciples set off for Rome, hoping that they would have an opportunity of presenting it to the Pope and of receiving his approval and his blessing. On arriving in Rome Francis seems, somehow or other, to have made his way alone into the Lateran palace where he encountered the Pope walking up and down one of the corridors. In his impulsive way he thrust the Rule under the Pope's nose and was told, rather brusquely, to go away.[2] Matthew Paris improves on this story by saying that the Pope told Francis to go and roll himself in the dirt with the pigs, and that Francis meekly obeyed. At any rate Francis realized that papal audiences were not to be had in that way, and looked around for some other method of winning the Pope's favour.

Alone in the great city of Rome this little band of enthusiasts would have small chance of achieving their purpose had not Francis, at this point, met the Bishop of Assisi who happened to be there at the time. He immediately took up their cause and introduced Francis to the Cardinal of S. Sabina who was one of the Pope's councillors. The Cardinal had several interviews with Francis, and at first tried to persuade him to enter one of the existing religious Orders or to become a hermit. But the saint was adamant in his purpose, and the Cardinal eventually saw that it was no good trying to deflect him from it, and so made arrangements for him to meet the Pope.

The day on which these two men met was one of the great days in the history of the Church. On one side was the young Francis, passionately keen to live this life to which he knew that he had been called but knowing that he could not go on

[1] Moorman, *Sources for the Life of S. Francis*, pp. 52ff.
[2] Bonaventura, *Legendae Duae S. Francisci* (ed. Quaracchi), pp. 28f.

unless he had official recognition, and on the other hand the great Pope Innocent III now in the twelfth year of his pontificate, shrewd, cautious, statesmanlike, disliking new Orders and "movements", and therefore anxious to get this young man and his friends into some existing organization. But though outwardly the two men appeared to represent two totally different points of view, fundamentally they were in agreement, for each desired above all else, that the will of God should be done and that the Church should be purified and strengthened.

Francis, therefore, produced his Rule and read it to the Pope and Cardinals, but it was rather coldly received. Everyone thought it too strict. No man could live that sort of life for long. Flesh and blood wouldn't stand it. There would inevitably be either relaxations or wholesale desertions. It was really fantastic to say that they should have no money at all and to expect intelligent and self-respecting men to go round from door to door with begging-bowls like tramps. This sort of thing had been tried before and it had always failed. Have a strict Rule, if you like; but let it be reasonable.

Francis' hopes must have sunk very low while all this was being said. But at this point two things happened. One was that the Cardinal of S. Sabina, who was Francis' only supporter in the curia, pointed out with devasting force that if they rejected this way of life, which was really nothing more than an attempt to live according to the Gospels, they would in fact be inferring that Christ did not know what he was talking about. "For", said the Cardinal, "if anyone shall say that in the observance of evangelical perfection, and the vow to keep it, there is contained anything new or irrational or impossible of observance, such a one is convicted of blasphemy against Christ, the Author of the Gospel."[1] The other thing which happened at this critical moment was that the Pope recalled a dream which he had recently had, in which he had seen the Church of St John Lateran falling down and a little man, poor and despised, had come up, put his shoulder under

[1] Bon: *Leg. Maj.*, iii, 9.

it and propped it up. He now suddenly identified the man before him as the man of his dream. These two incidents entirely changed the situation; the Pope became convinced that here was something genuine, a movement of the Spirit which nothing could stop, and he gave his sanction to the Rule and sent the shabby little party away with his blessing.

Francis had come to Rome as the leader of a band of penitents, he left it as the head of a religious Order. And from this point onwards the movement went ahead with great rapidity. Francis' dream in which he had seen the woods round the Portiuncula filled with strange faces as men came pouring in from France and from Spain, from Germany and from England soon began to come true. The friars, in their torn and patched habits, soon came to be a familiar sight not only on the roads of Italy but all over Europe. Nor was it long before missions were sent to North Africa, and even as far afield as India and China. By the latter part of the thirteenth century almost every town of any size had its community of Friars Minor. Within fifty years of the saint's death there were over fifty such communities in England alone, and more than five hundred in Italy.

Among the crowds who came were many men after St Francis' own heart. Of them all the one who was nearest to him and who became his closest friend was Brother Leo, the "little sheep of God", who joined the Order soon after they returned from Rome. It is to Brother Leo that we owe much of what we know of the saint, for he was constantly with him and, in later years, wrote his precious "rolls and notes" which were the stock out of which such works as the *Mirror of Perfection* and the *Second Life* by Thomas of Celano were written. Francis leaned much on Leo; and when the troubles began in the Order, and Francis' life was made miserable, it was to Leo that he confided his grief and from whom he received comfort and encouragement.

Closely associated with Brother Leo were the two friars who assisted in the writing of the reminiscences, Angelo Tancredi, the knight of Rieti, and Rufino, also of a noble family and cousin to St Clare. These two with Masseo, the tall and handsome, came to be among the inner circle of Francis' friends. But they were only part of a large family which contained some saints, a few sinners, and a large number of good men who saw in this movement a purity and zeal and devotion which they did not see elsewhere, and so threw in their lot with the poor friars in the hope that by so doing they could find a way of loyalty to Christ and service of his Church.

Two years after the visit to Rome, Francis was faced with a new problem, in some ways far more difficult than that of adapting himself to become the leader of a religious Order. In the spring of 1212 he had been preaching a series of sermons in the cathedral at Assisi, living meanwhile with a group of his companions, in some rough huts at the Portiuncula. Among those who listened to his preaching and who were deeply moved by it was a seventeen-year-old girl called Clare, of a noble family in Assisi. Not only had she listened to Francis' sermons but she had also had some opportunity of observing his work among the poor and the lepers and she formed a determination that she, too, would like to embrace a life of poverty and humility. Having developed what would nowadays be regarded as a not unusual adolescent passion for an older man, and being a girl of great strength of mind and determination, she decided to take matters into her own hands and throw herself at St Francis' feet. This project she seems to have discussed with the saint, but how far he was responsible for what subsequently happened it is difficult to say.

At any rate at night on Palm Sunday, 18 March, Clare escaped from her father's house, and made her way down the hill to the Portiuncula to the Order of Lesser Brothers. Before the altar of the little church she took some kind of simple vows, and Francis cut off her hair to show that she was now wedded to Christ.

When daylight came, and the excitement was over, Francis must have realized that he had presented himself with a very difficult problem. There can be little doubt that what Clare really wanted to do was to join the Order much on the same terms as the brethren. If she had merely wanted to enter a religious community there were plenty of nunneries which would have been only too glad to receive her. But she was not interested in the ordinary enclosed life of a nun. Just as Francis had consistently refused to join one of the existing orders because he knew that he must live and work in the crowded streets of the cities, among the poor and the sick and the unhappy, rather than behind the walls of a monastery, so Clare turned her back on the conventional religious life of women, hoping that she, too, would be able to go where men and women were starved both in soul and in body and bring light and peace. Surely some way could be found in which even a woman could join in this great work, not in any condescending way but by herself sharing in the privations of poverty and identifying herself with the poorest and most neglected.

Had she been born some centuries later this might have been possible. But in the thirteenth century there was no real opening for that kind of work. No one could accuse Francis of lack of originality or lack of courage, but to accept a woman into a community of men or to found an order of women evangelists was more than he could face. There was only one thing to be done: Clare must be lodged in one of the neighbouring Benedictine nunneries until arrangements could be made for her to have a convent of her own. So, after spending a few days at the Portiuncula while Francis went round looking for a suitable refuge, Clare was placed in a convent of Black Nuns at Bastia. Meanwhile preparations were made for the conversion of the church and buildings of St Damian's at Assisi into a religious house, and there, eventually, Clare and her younger sister Agnes were established. And there she remained until her death in 1253, having by then spent over forty years without having once gone outside the monastic enclosure.

How far all this was agreeable to St Clare we shall never

know. One of the qualities which stand out in her life is her obedience. Having once accepted Francis as her spiritual guide she was prepared to do whatever he told her to do. If it was his will that she should become an enclosed nun, then there was no more to be said about it. But one wonders whether there was not, deep down in her heart, a feeling of disappointment and of yearning for something more practical. Even if she could not go out as a preacher could she not have served the poor? or have nursed some colony of lepers? or even have ministered in some way to the friars? Perhaps she would have regarded these as evil thoughts. But it is recorded that when news reached her of five friars who had been martyred in Morocco she asked whether she might go and shed her blood for Christ.

In some ways the story of Clare must be regarded as a tragedy. She had great courage, deep devotion, and much strength of character, and she became a noble head of the first community of Poor Clares or Minoresses. But she was born out of her time. In more modern ages she could have enjoyed something of the freedom which is so essentially a part of the Franciscan ideal, especially the freedom which makes it possible for one to go where help is needed, to face hardship and danger in the cause of love, to bring hope and joy into lives which are otherwise squalid and hard and bitter. But to Clare in the thirteenth century, all this was denied. For her there was no alternative to the cloistered life. This, of course, had its own special virtues, but they were not the virtues which we particularly associate with the Franciscan ideal.

The coming of Clare gave Francis a new problem. Yet another was created, during the next few years, by the success of Francis' preaching. As the years went by he spent more and more of his time in preaching in various parts of Italy, and his fame began to spread. Crowds flocked to hear him and went away deeply impressed both by his message and by the quality of his life. The old days of persecution and misunderstanding gradually gave place to wild popularity. Francis came to be known as "the saint" and, wherever he went, large numbers came to see him and to hear him.

All this led to more and more candidates for the two Orders, the friars and the minoresses; but there were, of course, many, both men and women, who could not give up everything and enter upon the very strict life of those who were professed. Many were married folk and parents, some had responsibilities which they could not abandon or dependants whom they could not desert. Could anything be done for such people? Was there any method whereby they, too, could be drawn together into some kind of fellowship? Might they also, within their more limited spheres, consider themselves disciples of St Francis?

It was with such people in his mind that Francis, about the year 1214, wrote an "Open Letter to all the Faithful". He does not, in this letter, suggest any kind of society or fellowship, but he does lay down the principles upon which a religious life might be based. These include such things as a frequent reception of the Sacrament, regular confession, alms-giving, abstinence in food and drink, simplicity, humility, and love. Having laid down these Francis ends his letter with an exhortation:

> I, Brother Francis, your little servant, beg and beseech you by the Love which is God, and desiring to kiss your feet, that you will humbly and lovingly receive these fragrant words of our Lord Jesus Christ and cheerfully put them into practice and observe them to perfection. Let those who cannot read have them read to them often, and let them keep them with them and carry them out unto the end, for they are spirit and they are life.[1]

Those who accepted these standards, coming, as they did, from St Francis himself, soon began to form themselves into a loosely-knit body of penitents who adopted this simple rule of life as an act of loyalty to the saint. Thus there came into

[1] *Opusc.*, pp. 97f.

being, gradually and informally, the fellowship which was afterwards known as the "Third Order". For some years they had no title, no organization, and no Rule; they were held together only by their devotion to St Francis and their desire to put into practice in their own lives something of the spirit whereby he was inspired. But the numbers grew so great that some kind of organization became essential and about 1220 a formal Rule was drawn up by Francis and Cardinal Ugolino.

The order had now come to be called "The Brothers and Sisters of Penance" and the Rule was designed to set a standard of simplicity and devotion for men and women, clerks and lay folk, kings, bishops, nobles, and artisans who were prepared to regulate their lives, give up luxuries, say their prayers, and cultivate high standards of honesty. The Rule has a curiously Puritan or Quakerish ring about it, for the first clause gives minute regulations about the colour and quality of their clothes, which are to be drab and simple, and forbids them to attend banquets and plays. Other clauses give regulations about food—only two meals a day and special rules about fasting—about the saying of prayers, the times of confession and communion, the making of wills and acts of mercy and charity. Members of the Order were not allowed to bear arms, they were not to take oaths, and they were not to go to law before secular tribunals.

The Rule, therefore, was fairly exacting in its demands, but many were proud to embrace it. In time the Order could claim among its members such people as St Elizabeth of Hungary and St Louis of Toulouse, the great missionary Raymon Lull, and possibly Dante himself. Great work was done by its members in founding and serving hospitals and leper-houses, in introducing new standards of honesty into the business world, and in encouraging personal devotion; while the clothes and self-discipline of its members gave a perpetual challenge to the worldly.

Thus Francis' great family grew, and soon the whole of Italy and indeed the whole of Western Europe began to feel his influence. The friars became a familiar sight on the roads and in the churches, convents of Poor Clares were established in many towns, and everywhere were members of the so-called "Third Order" quietly witnessing, by the simplicity and goodness of their lives, to the inspiration which they had drawn from the Little Poor Man of Assisi.

4

The Apostolate

WHEN Francis and his little band of disciples returned from Rome after their interview with Innocent III they settled down not, as might have been expected, at the Portiuncula but in some partially ruined buildings at Rivo Torto close to the leper colony at Santa Maria Maddalena. The place was probably chosen because of its proximity to the lepers and also perhaps because of its poverty. The buildings were some more or less derelict wooden huts and were so small and cramped that the friars had scarcely room to sit down and Francis had to make chalk marks on the beams to indicate where each of the brothers might lie. Living conditions must indeed have been most uncomfortable, but Francis would have rejoiced to think that in this way they were serving the Lady Poverty.

Their time was fully occupied. There was, first of all, the time given to prayer. Francis has recorded that in these early days those who were clerks said their offices like other clerks, while the lay brothers were content with saying the Lord's Prayer.[1] But the shortage of books must have been a difficulty unless, as Francis suggests, they went and said their offices in some neighbouring church. Next came work—hard, manual work in the fields for which they would earn a little food though they were, of course, allowed to touch no money. As they were also forbidden to make any kind of bargain with the men for whom they worked, they were sometimes cheated or sent away empty-handed after a long day's toil, and it was then that they took their bowls and begged for their food "for the love of God". Then there was also the service of the lepers, washing their sores, keeping them and their squalid huts as

[1] *Opusc.*, p. 79.

clean as possible and trying to mitigate something of the pain and discomfort from which they suffered. Finally there was the work of evangelism. Francis was now beginning to preach, generally in the open air but occasionally in one of the churches in Assisi.

There is no doubt that life at Rivo Torto was very hard, so much so that the brothers found it almost more than they could bear. But Francis watched over them with the tenderest care. If he thought that they were tired or too sensitive to go begging he would go himself; if he thought they were suffering too greatly from hunger he would do his utmost to supply their need. Some of the friars, out of love of asceticism, used to cut down their food even below the standard imposed on them by necessity; but Francis never approved of this. Once, we are told, while they were still at Rivo Torto

it fell on a night, all the friars being at rest, about the middle of the night, one of them called out, saying, "I am dying!" Whereon all the friars woke up amazed and affrighted. And the holy father, rising, said, "Rise, brothers, and kindle the light!" And when it was lit he said: "Who is he that said 'I am dying'?" The brother answered: "It is I." And he said to him, "What is the matter, brother? How dost thou die?" And he said, "I am dying of hunger." Then the blessed father caused the table to be laid straightway, and like a man full of charity and discretion, ate with him lest he should be put to shame by eating alone; and, by his will, all the other friars ate likewise. For that brother, and all the other friars who had newly turned to the Lord, used to afflict their bodies even beyond measure. And after the meal the holy father said to the other friars: "Dearest, I bid you, each one, consider his nature, because though one of you may be able to sustain himself on less food, yet I will that another who requires more food shall not be bound to imitate the first in this thing, but shall, considering his own nature, give his body what it requires, so that it may be able to serve the spirit. For as we are bound to beware of superfluity of

64

eating, which harms the body and soul, so also must we beware of too great abstinence, nay, even more since the Lord will have mercy and not sacrifice. . . . Therefore I will and command you that each of our brethren, according to poverty, satisfy his body as it shall be necessary for him."[1]

This tender consideration is shown by another incident when Francis realized that one of the older brethren was afflicting himself more than was good for him

and he said within himself, "If that brother would eat some ripe grapes early in the morning I believe it would do him good." And as he thought, so he did. For he rose on a certain day, very early, and called to him that friar privately, and led him into a certain vineyard which was near the dwelling. And he chose a vine whereon the grapes were good to eat, and sitting near the vine with the friar, began to eat of the grapes lest the brother himself should be ashamed to eat alone. And while they were eating the friar was cured, and together they praised the Lord.[2]

So the months went by, and the work and the life went on. But obviously they could not stay here for ever. Poor and wretched and cramped though they were these old huts were becoming a "home", and the friars must have no place of their own, since the Son of Man had had nowhere to lay his head. The friars were, therefore, by no means disappointed when a peasant appeared one day with his ass and drove the beast into the hovel crying, "Get in with you, get right in; for we shall do well in this place".[3] Francis took this as a sign that they must be on the move, and they immediately left their shabby little home and began to travel further afield.

From this point onwards the friars were constantly moving about the country, the only stipulation being that they should gather together once a year, at Whitsuntide, at the Portiuncula for their annual Chapter. Of all places this was most dear to Francis, for it was here that he had finally made his decision

---

[1] *Spec.* 27. [2] *Spec.* 28. [3] 3 *Soc.* 55.

to follow in the footsteps of Christ. "This place", says Celano, "the saint loved above all others, this he bade his brethren respect with special reverence, this he willed ever to be kept as the mirror of the Religion in the utmost humility and poverty, reserving the property therein to others and retaining but the use of it for himself and his brethren."[1] The little chapel belonged to the Benedictine monks of Subasio from whom Francis received permission to use it, though, in order to show that the friars had no real possession of it, a basket of fish was paid as rent each year to the monks. Around the church a circle of huts was built out of mud and branches; and, in so far as the friars came to have any place which they would regard as "home", this was it. Francis dearly loved it and everything about it—its name, its simplicity, its position hidden away in the woods, its associations with the days of his conversion and the early adventures of the friars. Later, when the Pope had granted an indulgence to all who visited it, it became a place of pilgrimage to which people came from all over the world, and it stands to-day sheltered by the great church of Santa Maria degli Angeli which has been built over it, but still retaining something of its primitive simplicity.

But Francis would not allow the friars to stay there long. Their true work was among the people, on the roads, in the cities and villages, in the fields and vineyards where there was work to be done. The Portiuncula might be a place to which a friar could come for rest and refreshment and new inspiration, but it was not meant to serve as a permanent home for any. So the little company split up into small groups and scattered, north, south, east, and west, to bear the message of the Gospel and to preach the virtues of poverty, humility, and simplicity, and this by their lives just as much as by their words. At first these missionary journeys were confined to the neighbourhood, but the friars soon went further afield, south to the Valley of Rieti and to Rome itself, eastward to the Marches of Ancona, northwards to Florence and Bologna. Once Francis penetrated into Spain, and he made more than

[1] 2 *Cel.* 18.

one effort to reach France, the land whose language he spoke and whose literature he loved, though it is doubtful whether he ever succeeded in getting there. So the friars pursued their way, tramping from village to village and from town to town, working with their hands, begging their food, serving the lepers, and, above all, preaching the Gospel. With such zeal did they set about their work that it is recorded that Francis sometimes managed to preach in as many as four or five villages or towns in one day.

And always as they went, they maintained the highest standards of poverty. Often they were so famished that they had to beg for turnips out of the fields to stave off the pangs of hunger. A story of the early days tells how Francis and Bernard came to one town, tired and hungry, and set out to go and beg a few scraps of food, agreeing to meet again by a certain stone. When they came together again in the evening light, Francis had the crusts which he had been given, but Bernard had nothing—he had been so hungry that he had been unable to wait, and had eaten the lot. Then Francis "wept for joy and, embracing Brother Bernard, cried out with a loud voice, 'Indeed, my sweetest son, you are a much holier man than I am. You are perfect follower of the holy Gospel, for you have laid up no store, neither have you taken any thought for the morrow, but you have cast all your care upon God.' "[1]

Often, too, they were insulted and persecuted. The further afield they went the less likely were they to be known, and where they were not known they were liable to be suspected. The poor friars who went to Germany in 1219 probably had the roughest time of any. They were totally ignorant of the language of the country but discovered that by answering "Ja" to the questions which were put to them they were often given food and shelter, so they decided that this was a magic word which they would always employ. But when they cheerfully replied "Ja" to one who asked them if they were heretics they soon found themselves roughly handled, beaten, stripped, and cast into prison. In Hungary the shepherds set their dogs

[1] *A New Fior.*, p. 20f.

on them, drove them away with their pikes and stole their scanty garments.[1]

But still the work went on, still the sheep went out among the wolves, and at the centre of it all was the frail little figure of St Francis, burning with zeal, tireless, and fearless, a living expression of the gospel of love which he so ardently preached. Thomas of Celano, who knew him personally, has given a description of what the saint looked like. He writes:

He was of middle height, inclining to shortness; his head was of moderate size and round; his face somewhat long and prominent, his forehead smooth and small; his eyes were black, of moderate size, and with a candid look; his hair was dark, his eyebrows straight, his nose symmetrical, thin and straight, his ears upright but small, his temples smooth. His words were kindly, but fiery and penetrating; his voice was powerful, sweet-toned, clear and sonorous. His teeth were set close together, white and even; his lips thin and fine, his beard black and rather scanty, his neck slender; his shoulders straight, his arms short, his hands attenuated, with long fingers and nails; his legs slight, his feet small, his skin fine, and his flesh very spare.[2]

Such was the outward appearance of the little man who was turning the world upside down by his preaching. On arrival in a parish he would first ask permission to preach to the people. If this were given he would begin without delay either in the church or in the *piazza*; if it were not given he would generally go on sadly to the next village, hoping for better things. Once when he came to the city of Imola he went to the bishop and asked permission to preach.

The bishop replied: "Brother, it is enough for *me* to preach to my people." St Francis bowed his head and humbly went out; but after a short time he came back again: "What do you want now, brother?" said the bishop; "what are you seeking now?" And the blessed Francis replied: "My lord,

[1] *Chron. Jordani*, 5f.   [2] *I Cel.* 83.

68

when a father has driven a son out of one door he must come in again by another." The bishop, conquered by this humility, embraced him with glad looks, and said: "You and all your brothers may in future take my general licence to preach in this diocese, for this holy humility of yours has earned this privilege."[1]

Often Francis had to preach in the open air and this sometimes led to disturbances whether intentional or otherwise. Perhaps of all places in which he preached Perugia was the most difficult, for there was an old feeling of enmity between the citizens of Assisi and Perugia, and it was not to be wondered at that when a man who had once borne arms against the people of Perugia appeared in their city as a herald of the gospel of peace a party of young knights should have done their best to wreck the sermon by careering about the cobbled square on their horses, scattering the people right and left and drowning the voice of the preacher. But Francis turned on them and prophesied terrible things for them, which, say the legends, were duly fulfilled.[2] Equally successful was he in silencing a flock of swallows which twittered so loudly while he was preaching at Alviano that he had to break off and ask the birds to be quiet until he had finished his sermon,[3] and a similar incident took place with an unruly ass at Trevi.[4]

Not one of Francis' sermons has survived, nor is this altogether surprising for he spoke very much "as the Spirit gave him utterance". One man, a "natural philosopher", after hearing Francis speak on many occasions said: "Whereas I can remember every word of the sermons of others the words uttered by holy Francis alone escape me." And he added sadly: "If I commit any of them to memory they do not seem to me the same that fell from his lips before."[5] That they were delivered with much passion and fervour is certain, and their effect upon people was sometimes startling. Celano, who had probably heard Francis preach, speaks of his introducing

[1] 2 Cel. 147.   [2] Spec. 105.   [3] 1 Cel. 59.
[4] A New Fior., p. 68.   [5] 2 Cel. 107.

"ardent gestures and movements", and on the famous occasion when he preached before the Pope and Cardinals we know that he got so excited that he began to dance, and the Lord Ugolino, who had arranged for the sermon to be given, was terrified that the Sacred Congregation would burst out laughing.[1] But people did not generally laugh when Francis was preaching; they were far more likely to cry. His whole appearance, the absolute sincerity behind those shining eyes, the simplicity and fearlessness of his life and the effects of his self-discipline showing in his body were enough to move most people to tears.

Sometimes his sermons took a highly unconventional turn. There was, for example, the famous occasion when he ordered Brother Rufino to go and preach in Assisi. But Rufino, knowing himself to be a very poor preacher, begged to be excused, whereupon Francis was angry with him for not obeying a command, and ordered him to go "naked as thou wast born, save in thy breeches only". So the poor Rufino, of the house of the Scifi and related to all the best people in Assisi, solemnly entered one of the churches in the town with nothing on but his drawers and began his sermon. As might have been expected the sermon was not a success, for no one could keep a straight face, and even the most charitable thought that Rufino's mind had been affected by his austerities. Meanwhile Francis became overwhelmed with shame and contrition at having imposed so hard a penance on Brother Rufino and he cried out: "Whence comes to thee such boldness, thou son of Peter Bernardone, vile wretch, to command Brother Rufino, that is one of the most noble gentles of Assisi, to go and preach to the people like a madman? By God, thou shalt have proof in thine own self of what thou biddest others do." So Francis then stripped himself and made his way to the church where poor Rufino was attempting to preach his sermon. The laughter now increased, but Francis went into the pulpit "and began to preach so marvellously of contempt of the world, of holy penitence, of voluntary poverty, of the

[1] I *Cel.* 73.

desire of the Kingdom of heaven, and of the nakedness and shame of the passion of our Lord Jesus Christ, that all they that heard the preaching, men and women in great multitude, began to weep most bitterly with devout and contrite hearts; and not there alone, but in all Assisi was there that day much weeping for the passion of Christ, that never had there been the like."[1]

On another occasion, when he was due to preach to the Poor Clares at St Damian's, Francis suddenly refused to preach at all. It was only after a great deal of persuasion that he had consented to preach to the nuns, but

> when the ladies were gathered together as usual to hear the word of God (but not less in order to see their father) he raised his eyes to heaven, where his heart ever was, and began to pray to Christ. Then he ordered ashes to be brought, and having spread some of them on the ground in a circle round him, placed the remainder on his head. They waited for him to begin, but as he remained in persistent silence within the circle of ashes, no small astonishment arose in their hearts. Then the saint suddenly stood up, and to their amazement repeated, by way of sermon, the Psalm: "Have mercy upon me, O God", and having finished it went out in haste.[2]

His preaching was certainly unaccountable: no one ever knew what was going to happen. If he had thought out what he was going to say the chances were that when the time came he would have completely forgotten what he had prepared. On one of the occasions when Francis preached before the curia at Rome, Cardinal Ugolino was so fearful that he would not be up to the occasion that he sat up all night writing out a sermon for him. Poor Ugolino! he little knew his man. As might have been expected Francis entirely forgot what he had been told to say and, being at a loss what to do, he opened a psalter and, lighting on the verse: "My confusion is daily before me, and the shame of my face hath covered me", he

[1] *Fior.* 30.   [2] 2 *Cel.* 207.

used this as a text for a fiery discourse on the sins of the hierarchy.[1] On other occasions when he really was at a loss what to say he would just dismiss the people with his blessing.

As he went his way he often met crowds of people and he loved to speak to them, combining real eloquence with a quickness to seize any opportunity. He once came to the castle of Montefeltro in 1213 and found the place in *festa*. The courtyard was filled with people, and it looks as if some singer had just sung one of the romantic songs of the troubadours in which the weary crusader thinks of his mistress and cries:

> So great the good I have in sight
> That every pain I count delight.

Immediately Francis leapt on to a low wall, took these words as his text, and preached so convincingly on asceticism and the joys of heaven that he held the crowd spellbound.[2] Francis may not have been a very striking person to look at, but as soon as he opened his mouth men began to feel his power. One contemporary account of his preaching has survived, that of Thomas of Spalato who heard him preach at Bologna in 1222. "His tunic", he says, "was dirty, his person unprepossessing and his face far from handsome; but God gave such power to his words that many factions of the nobility, among whom the fierce anger of ancient feuds had been raging with much bloodshed, were brought to reconciliation. Towards him, indeed, the reverence and devotion of men were so great that men and women rushed upon him headlong, anxious to touch the hem of his garment and to carry away bits of his clothing."[3]

As Francis travelled about the country he also had many opportunities of giving personal advice to people who were in trouble or difficulty, though he never stayed long enough in one place to exercise any kind of pastoral ministry. All that side of the work he was content to leave to the parish priests

[1] *A New Fior.*, p. 44.   [2] *Fio.*   1st Consid. of Stigmata.
[3] *A New Fior.*, p. 63.

with whom he was always anxious to co-operate. But it was inevitable that after one of his sermons people should wish to approach him not only to carry away bits of his clothing but also of his advice. Sometimes those who came to him were young men who wanted to be received into the Order. Francis had a remarkable instinct for knowing when a vocation was genuine and when it was not. One young gentleman of Lucca who knelt before Francis with tears in his eyes imploring to be allowed to join the friars received the reply: "Miserable and carnal boy, why do you think that you can lie to the Holy Spirit and to me? Your weeping is carnal and your heart is not with God. Go, for you savour of nothing spiritual."[1] Another who, having been told to distribute his goods to the poor, gave them all to his relations, was greeted with the words: "Go your way, Brother Fly, for you have not yet left your house and kindred. You have given your goods to your relatives and have defrauded the poor; you are not, therefore, worthy to live with the holy poor."[2] On the other hand Francis was quick to see real goodness and sincerity, as he did in Brother John the Simple whom he accepted at sight and was accustomed afterwards to refer to not as "Brother John" but as "Saint John".[3] Many stories are told of Francis' penetration and of his uncanny power of reading the thoughts of others. Friars who made a show of great holiness sometimes received very severe rebukes, and a canon who in great sickness asked the saint to bless him received the reply: "Since you have lived in the past according to the lusts of the flesh without fearing God's judgments, how can I sign you with the cross?"[4] Others were startled, and sometimes dismayed, to find Francis perfectly aware of what they were thinking.

A visit of St Francis, or of one of the leading friars, to a little town was likely to be an event of great importance, an importance which grew as the Order became better known. First the saint would preach to the people; then there would be interviews and talks, discussions and arguments, then

[1] 2 *Cel.* 40.   [2] 2 *Cel.* 81.
[3] *Spec.* 57.   [4] 2 *Cel.* 41.

73

almost certainly the healing of the sick. Thus gradually the hostility and suspicion of the early days gave place to love and friendship and Francis' evangelistic marches became triumphal journeys since he was heralded everywhere with acclamation. Celano is hardly exaggerating when he says: "If he entered any city the clergy were joyful, the bells were rung, the men exulted, the women rejoiced together, and children clapped their hands and often took boughs of trees and went in procession to meet him singing psalms."[1]

In cold or wet weather Francis generally managed to find some kind of shelter at night, but in summertime he often slept out in the open. This open-air life, combined with his affectionate spirit and his perpetual contemplation of the works of the Creator, brought him into a specially close relationship with nature. All that he saw as he walked the countryside—earth and sky, animals and birds, trees and flowers—all were part of the mighty creative work of God, and were, therefore "very good". That he should regard the creatures of God as his brothers and sisters was perfectly natural; they were a part of the world in which he lived, sharing the good things which God provided for all that he had made. Moreover, unlike many of his fellow countrymen, he had very strong feelings about the rights of all living creatures. Animals, he would have said, are no more created by God to minister to the needs of man than man is to the needs of animals. Man must eat what God provides—and even Francis was no vegetarian—but he has no right to kill animals unnecessarily, and any kind of cruelty is an outrage against God.

Thus the first thing which we notice about St Francis and the natural world is a great tenderness. We are told that he used to pick up worms out of the way lest they should be trodden under the foot of man, and that he wished a law to be made that all should provide special food for the birds and for all beasts of burden at Christmas time. Once when he was in the Marches of Ancona

[1] 1 *Cel.* 62.

he met a man carrying two lambs, bound and hanging over his shoulders, which he was taking to market to sell. When the blessed Francis heard them bleating he was moved with compassion, and came near and touched them, showing pity for them like a mother towards her crying child. And he said to the man: "Why do you thus torment my brother lambs by carrying them bound and hanging like this?" And the man replied: "I am taking them to market to sell, for I must get a price for them." "What will become of them afterwards?" said the saint. "Whoever buys them will kill and eat them." "God forbid," said the holy man, "this must not be; take the cloak I am wearing in exchange for them and give them to me." The man gave him the lambs and took the cloak gladly, for it was of much greater value. (St Francis had borrowed it that day from a faithful man to keep off the cold.) When he had received the lambs he carefully considered what he should do with them, and after consulting with his companion he gave them back to the man, charging him never to sell them or do them hurt, but to keep them, feed them, and take good care of them.[1]

This compassion, this feeling that all things had their rights which must be respected, was extended far beyond such creatures as lambs and birds to include the less attractive parts of the creation and even inanimate things such as fire. Once when Francis was sitting by the fire his hose got alight and one of the friars rushed up to put it out, but the saint did his utmost to forbid him; why should Brother Fire be defrauded of his rights? On another occasion a hut in which Francis was living caught fire and before the place was completely destroyed he picked up some clothes and carried them to a place of safety. But he was afterwards overcome with remorse and informed the friars that he would never wear those garments again since, by rescuing them, he had robbed Brother Fire of his food.

The extreme sensitiveness of his feelings about nature and

[1] 1 *Cel.* 79.

the intimacy of his relationship with the creation led to his having a peculiar power over all living things. There is no story more popular or more beloved than the story of how St Francis, passing near Bevagna, came upon a large flock of birds and, finding to his surprise that they did not fly away when he approached them, preached to them that they should praise God and be thankful for all that he gives them.[1] Wild animals seem to have had no fear of him and when, after fondling them, he wanted to get rid of them, he often found great difficulty in persuading them to go away. The flock of swallows which interrupted his preaching at Alviano was silenced by a word from the saint, and a hawk at La Verna became his "knocker-up" and woke him for Mattins each morning. Wolves and other wild beasts gave him no fear and became perfectly docile in his company, while the fierce wolf of Gubbio became so tame that it lived to be quite a popular figure in the town and died universally mourned.

But though Francis had an affection for all created things his feelings were specially aroused where some association could be found between the creature and Christ. We are told for example, that he used to walk over rocks with the utmost reverence since the psalmist speaks of the Lord as his "strong rock". Trees he specially loved because of the cross, and he could not bear to see lights put out, since Christ called himself the "Light of the World". Lambs were, naturally, particularly dear to him because of the "Lamb of God", and there is a most beautiful story of how the saint and Brother Paul were travelling near Osimo when they found a shepherd feeding a flock of goats in a field.

Among the multitude of goats there was one little sheep going along in humble fashion and quietly grazing. When Francis saw her he stopped, and, moved in his heart with grief, said to the brother who accompanied him, groaning aloud: "Seest thou not this sheep which is walking so meekly among these she-goats? I tell thee that even so our Lord Jesus

[1] 1 *Cel.* 58, etc.

76

Christ walked meek and lowly among the Pharisees and Chief Priests. Wherefore I ask thee, my son, for love of Him, to take pity with me on this little sheep, and let us pay the price and get her out from among these goats." And Brother Paul, wondering at his grief, began to grieve with him. But they had nothing but the poor tunics they wore. And as they were anxiously considering how the price might be paid, a merchant who was on a journey came up and offered the price they desired. They took the sheep, giving thanks to God and came to Osimo: and went in to the bishop of that city, who received them with great reverence. The Lord bishop, however, wondered both at the sheep which the man of God was leading, and at the affection wherewith he was moved toward her. But after Christ's servant had unfolded to him at some length the parable of the sheep, the bishop, pricked at the heart, gave thanks to God for the purity of the man of God. Next day, on leaving the city, Francis considered what he should do with the sheep, and by his companion's advice he handed it over to a monastery of the handmaids of Christ at San Severino to be taken care of. The venerable handmaids of Christ received the sheep with joy as a great gift bestowed on them by God, and they kept it carefully for a long time, and wove of the wool a tunic which they sent to the blessed father Francis at the church of S. Maria de Portiuncula on the occasion of a Chapter. The saint of God received it with great reverence and exaltation of mind, and embraced it and kissed it again, and again, inviting all the bystanders to share his joy.[1]

All this side of St Francis' nature is very attractive to the modern mind and especially to us English people who are inclined to be rather sentimental about animals and birds. No artist feels that he has done justice to St Francis unless he has depicted him surrounded by flocks of birds and some of the more attractive of the wild mammals, and the saint has become the unofficial patron of various animal welfare societies.

[1] 1 *Cel.* 77f.

Now there is, of course, no harm whatever in this so long as we are quite clear in our minds about three things. First, St Francis' love of creatures grew out of his love of God, and not vice versa. It was not through nature that he found God, still less did he substitute for true religion a kind of pantheism; his whole life was completely absorbed by the thought of the love of God, and his love of the created proceeded directly from his love of the Creator. Secondly, his love for created things was all-embracing, the only creatures for which he had a special affection being not those which are naturally attractive but those which were in some way associated with Christ. Artists should take note of this, for, to do justice to St Francis, they should include in their pictures not only doves and squirrels, but rats and toads and even bugs and lice. Thirdly, Francis' interest in nature and his love for all wild things was only second to his love for man, and his preaching to the birds was something which he would have regarded as an unimportant incident compared with his preaching of the Gospel to men and women. Francis was pre-eminently an evangelist not a naturalist, his life was dedicated to the service of God and the winning of souls to greater love and obedience; other interests were but a background to that work, a source of joy and satisfaction in their way but not to be compared in importance with the ministry of reconciliation. If Francis could choose the sort of stained-glass window which he would like to be erected in his memory he would certainly choose one which depicted him surrounded not by birds and butterflies, but by the sick and the leprous, by cripples and tramps, by all the dregs of society whose life he so bravely shared and whose souls he so dearly loved.

Next in importance to the preaching of the Gospel was the necessity for manual work in the life of the friar. So much has been said of Francis' dependence upon begging for his daily needs that it is not always realized that the quest for alms was only a last resort when other methods of getting their food had failed. In his Testament Francis writes: "I used to work with my hands and I wish so to work. And I would have all the other brothers work at some task so long as it is honest. Those who don't know how to work should learn, not from any desire to earn a reward but for an example to others and to avoid idleness. And when the reward of our labour is not given to us let us go to the table of the Lord and seek alms from door to door."[1] With this we may compare the earliest Rule in which it is laid down as follows: "Those brothers who know how to work shall work and pursue whatever trade they have learnt. . . . And *when necessary* let them go begging like the other brethren",[2] and Celano tells us that "no one could appear before the saint idle without receiving a sharp reprimand. For he himself, the pattern of all perfection, used to work and labour with his hands, suffering naught of that best gift of time to run to waste."[3]

It is important, therefore, to realize that the Friars Minor were first and foremost an order of *labourers* rather than an order of *mendicants*, though this is what they became as time went on. In this insistence upon manual work Francis was very much in line with other founders of religious Orders, the difference being that the work of the friars lay in the countryside as a whole, not within the precincts of a monastery. As the friars went about, they were, therefore, to look for work, and if they had any special craft for which they were trained they were to exercise it. We must therefore imagine friars acting as smiths and cooks and plumbers and ploughmen doing quite skilled jobs and thereby earning their keep. The primitive Rule suggests that many of the early friars did in fact live in private houses where they worked as house-boys and scullions, while many also worked in the fields and vineyards. Francis himself made it his job to go round sweeping out churches which had been neglected, for which purposes he for a long time carried a broom with him. Brother Giles earned special praise for his energy in working with his hands. When living in Rome he used to go out early in the morning

[1] *Opusc.*, p. 79.   [2] See above, p. 52.   [3] 2 *Cel.* 161.

to a wood eight miles from the city to carry sticks which he exchanged for bread. Or he would spend the day gathering olives, or gleaning, or treading the wine-press, or beating walnut trees. "Seldom", we are told, "did he work the whole day through, for he always bargained to have some space of time to say the canonical hours and not to fail in his mental prayers", and so often as not he seems to have given to the poor most of what he earned.

As time went on, and the Order became more settled and more organized, there was a tendency for such labour to be abandoned. But the original intentions of St Francis are clear enough, and in so far as the character of the Order changed it did so against his will.

If a friar were unable to get work, or if he were so much occupied in preaching or in ministering to the lepers that he had no time for manual work, or if for the work which he did the reward was insufficient for his simple needs he must have recourse to "the table of the Lord"—that is to say, he must take his bowl and beg for his food from door to door. That some of the early friars found this a most disagreeable task is easily understood, and Francis was so sensitive to their feelings that he himself used often to go alone to beg food for the whole brotherhood. But this became too great a burden for him to bear, and as the friars did not offer to help, he was obliged to send them out. "Dearest brothers and my little children," he said,

be not ashamed to go, for this is our heritage which our Lord Jesus Christ acquired and left to us and to all who wish by His example to live in holy poverty. In truth I say to you, that many of the noble and more holy of this world shall come to this congregation, and shall hold it for great honour and grace to go and seek alms. Go, therefore, confident in mind and rejoicing with the benediction of God, for alms. And you ought the more willingly and rejoicingly to go for alms than he who for one piece of money should return a hundred pence, since you offer to them from whom you seek an alms the love of God, saying: "For the love of God, do us an alms-deed", in comparison with Whom heaven and earth are as naught.[1]

Then the friars went out gladly and competed with one another as to which of them could collect the most.

In the mind of St Francis food collected as alms was more precious than anything else because it had been given "for the love of God". Consequently, even when there was no need to go begging Francis would sometimes go out and bring home scraps and morsels of food which he treated with the utmost reverence. He would do this even when staying in the house of the great. For example, when he was once a guest in the house of Cardinal Ugolino, Bishop of Ostia,

> at dinner-time he went out as if by stealth for alms from door to door. And when he returned, my lord of Ostia had already gone in to dinner with many knights and nobles. But the blessed Francis drew near and placed the alms which he had received on the table beside him, for the bishop desired the blessed father always to sit near him. And the Cardinal was a little ashamed because Francis had gone for alms and put them on the table; but he said nothing to him because of the guests. And when the blessed Francis had eaten a little he took of his alms and sent a little to each of the knights and chaplains of my Lord Cardinal on behalf of the Lord God. . . . And some did eat but others put it aside out of their great devotion to him.

After the meal Ugolino told Francis that he ought not to have gone out in this way, but Francis defended himself saying:

> Being with you, who are our lord and our apostle, and with other magnates and rich men of the world, who for the love of the Lord God not only receive me with much devotion into your houses, but also compel me to sit at your table, I will not be ashamed to beg alms; nay, I would fain have and

[1] *Spec.* 18.

hold this a very great nobility and royal dignity before God, and in honour of Him who, though He was Lord of all, wished for our sakes to become the servant of all, and though He was rich and glorious in His Majesty became poor and despised in our humility.

Then he added: "The bread of charity is holy bread which the praise and love of the Lord God sanctifies."[1] And that explains why St Francis regarded begging as so important. Far from being just a disagreeable necessity it was a glorious privilege, for in his eyes the crusts which the friars collected were imbued with a sacramental value; they had become "holy bread", blessed and sanctified by Love.

In addition to identifying themselves with the beggars of this world by going for alms the early friars maintained a high standard of poverty. If they had any buildings of their own they were always of the simplest. At the Portiuncula they built a few huts out of the branches of trees; at the Carceri they lived in caves hollowed out of the rock; at other places they built themselves hovels of clay and wattles. Francis was always most eager that such buildings as they had should be of the very simplest in order that the Lady Poverty might be honoured and her wishes observed. Even when the Order grew and it became essential for the friars to have some permanent centres for their work, Francis insisted that their homes should be very poor and simple. If some well-wisher gave them land on which to build they were first to obtain permission from the bishop and then, having received his blessing,

let them go and make a great trench in the circuit of the land which they have received for building the dwelling, and let them set there a good hedge as their wall, as a sign of holy poverty and humility. Afterwards let them make poor little houses of wattle and daub, and some little cells in which from time to time the friars may pray and work, for greater seemliness and to avoid sloth. Let them also

[1] *Spec.* 23.

build small churches for they ought not to make great churches, neither to preach to the people nor for any other reason, since their humility is greater and their example better when they go to other churches to preach. And if at any time prelates and clergy, regular or secular, come to their dwellings, the poor little houses, the little cells, and the tiny churches will preach to them, and they will be more edified by them, than by words.[1]

Within these humble little buildings everything was of the simplest: the friars had no beds but only a little straw on the bare earth, and they ate their food sitting on the ground since they were without tables and chairs. They had no libraries, no treasures, no vestments or ornaments in their tiny chapels, all was cut down to a minimum in order that " everything might sing of pilgrimage and exile".[2] And with the minimum of buildings and furniture went also the minimum of food and clothes. Francis always wished that every friar, like himself, should wear only a simple tunic with cord and breeches; and though, as time went on, he was forced to make certain relaxations in this rule, they were always made against his better judgement and he consistently refused to take advantage of them himself, even though, for many years, he was ill and weak. For although Francis told the brethren to "beware of too great abstinence" he had no mercy on his own body, and Celano is bound to admit that at this point the saint's preaching did not correspond with his practice. So little mercy had he for his own body that at the end of his life he was forced to admit that he had been very hard on poor Brother Ass, the unhappy beast who had had the burden of carrying his soul about for forty years or more and who had been often starved and beaten by his exacting master.

Poverty, austerity, privation, and asceticism—these were the marks of the early Franciscans as they went about the world preaching the gospel of love and striving to act as "mirrors of perfection". But Francis was insistent that the hard-

[1] *Spec.* 10.   [2] 2 *Cel.* 60.

ships which they endured—whether voluntary or of necessity —should never be allowed to quench joy. Self-pity, moroseness, despondency were things which the true Christian must never show. Second only to love in the nine fold "Fruit of the Spirit" stands joy; and Francis endeavoured, both by his example and by his teaching, to impress upon all men, and especially upon his own disciples, the duty of cultivating a joyful spirit. Brother Leo tells us that Francis was constantly urging the friars to cultivate the quality of "spiritual gladness" and that he often reproved them for sadness and outward grief. "For he used to say that if the servant of God would study to preserve within and without the spiritual joy which comes from cleanness of heart and is acquired by devoutness of prayer, the devils would not be able to harm him, for they would say, 'Since this servant of God has joy in tribulation as well as in prosperity, we can find no way of entering into him nor of hurting him.'" And he once blamed one of the friars who had a melancholy appearance, saying to him: "Why do you make an outward show of sorrow and sadness for your sins? Keep such sadness between yourself and God, and pray to Him that, by His mercy, He may spare you and restore to your soul the gladness of His salvation which you have lost through sin; but before me and others try always to be joyful, for it is not fitting that a servant of God should show before his brother, or others, sadness or a troubled face."[1]

But Brother Leo then goes on to say that he does not wish to be misunderstood or to convey the impression that Francis was ever hilarious or flippant. Far from it. In fact, he says, Francis "singularly abhorred laughing and idle words in the servant of God, since not only did he wish that he should not laugh, but that he should not even afford to others the slightest occasion for laughing". It is important to remember this for it is sometimes thought that Francis went about the world with the intention of making people happy. On the contrary; his main object was to make people repent and be sorry for

[1] *Spec.* 95f.

their sins. There was, therefore, a seriousness about his life and his preaching which people sometimes found most uncomfortable. The modern sects which go about trying to spread jollity and cheerfulness would have found no support in St Francis. The cross and human sin meant far too much to him, and he was always far nearer to tears than to laughter.

The same austerity comes out in the saint's attitude towards women. He once remarked that there were only two women in the world whom he knew by sight, and it is generally thought that these were St Clare and the Roman lady Jacomina de' Settesoli. He always avoided looking a woman in the face, and when he was obliged to speak to one he kept his eyes on the ground or gazed up at the sky; and he told the friars that "all talk with women is worthless except only in the way of confession or the very brief admonition that is customary".[1]

It is important to remember these facts about St Francis as recorded by those who knew him intimately, for there has often been a tendency to try to make him fit into a mould of our own design instead of listening to what his contemporaries have to say about him. The modern eye is fascinated by the picture of a man who went about talking to the birds and picking up worms from the roads, who broke away from all the usual forms of ecclesiasticism and preached a gospel of love without caring much about dogma, who was always doing whimsical things, who was friendly to all—men, women and children—and who made it his object to cheer people up and bring smiles and laughter where he found sorrow and unhappiness. Nothing could be further from the truth, and if we are to understand this most lovable of saints we must try to see him as he was and not as we should like him to have been.

There was, in fact, a sternness about St Francis which is often overlooked or deliberately suppressed. I once heard a lady exclaim: "Ah, if only St Francis could come back to us", but I could not help wondering whether she would really care

[1] *2 Cel.* 112ff.

to have him in her elegant drawing-room if her wish had been fulfilled. For one thing he would have refused to look at her at all; he would also have brought with him an air of dirt and squalor, especially if he had come straight from the leper-house or the slums; and, finally, he would most probably have spoken to her about her sins in a way which she would have thought both personal and uncalled for. Much as we love St Francis we must not shut our eyes to the fact that there is something frightening about him, about his absolute standards and about his uncompromising teaching. In some ways we get nearer to the real St Francis in Berlinghieri's stern and for-bidding figure,[1] than in the kindly old gentleman of the Giotto frescoes.

But the task of the evangelist, undertaken with such courage and such fire, was taking its toll of Francis' strength. The more he preached the more people needed his help and the less time he had for his own spiritual life and prayers. With heroic zeal he sacrificed more and more of his rest in order to find time for his devotions, often, after a long day of tramping and preaching, retiring to some church or into the woods to spend the whole night in prayer. But flesh and blood could not stand this for long. Gradually it became more and more clear to him that he must choose whether to go on with the active life of an evangelist or whether to retire to some hermitage and devote what was left of his earthly life to prayer and con-templation. The question troubled his mind for some time and eventually he decided to seek the advice of two whose word he could trust—St Clare and Brother Silvester. So he called Brother Masseo and said to him: "Go to sister Clare and bid her from me that she and some of the most spiritual of her companions pray devoutly unto God that He may be pleased to reveal to me which is the more excellent way: whether to give myself up to preaching or wholly to prayer. Then go to Brother Silvester and bid him do the like." Masseo went and delivered his message, but each gave the same reply:

[1] Reproduced in *S. Francis: Essays in Commemoration*, ed. W. Seton, p. 8.

86

"Go to Brother Francis and tell him that God has not called him just for his own benefit, but that he may bring forth fruit of souls and that, through him, many may be saved."[1]

From the moment of receiving this clear response Francis knew what he must do. He had given himself to God, and God was now giving him to the people. And from this point he never looked back, never again doubted the divine commission. "Forthwith", says St Bonaventura in describing this incident, "he rose and girded himself and without delay set forth on his journey. And with such fervour did he go to fulfil the divine command, and with such speed did he hasten on his way, that he seemed—the hand of the Lord being upon him—to have put on new power from on high."[2]

[1] *Fior.* 16.   [2] Bon: *Leg. Maj.*, xii, 2

5

Crisis in the Order

FOLLOWING up the advice of Clare and Silvester, Francis threw himself with renewed vigour into his missionary and evangelistic work. In its earlier stages this had been confined to the country of his birth, but Francis was aware also of the call of the non-Christian races, and especially of the Moslems. In the twelfth and thirteenth century the Church in the West had become vividly conscious of the menace of the advance of Islam and vigorous counteraction had been taken. Francis had grown up in the great crusading era. As a child he must have heard stories of the Third Crusade and of the emperors and kings who took part in it—Frederick Barbarossa, Richard Cœur-de-lion, and Philip of France—and no doubt he dreamed of one day going out with the crusaders to do battle for the Cross.

But he was now engaged in quite another kind of battle for the cross, a battle to be fought not "with swords and with staves" but by preaching the words of Christ and by setting an example of Christian living. If this battle could be fought in the lanes and streets of Italy, could it not be fought also in the land of the Saracens? If he, Christ's disciple and missionary, could once reach the Moslem hosts why should he not preach the Gospel to them? And if God gave him success, then there would be no need for any further crusades; the battle would be won. Moreover, if he failed and lost his life, what could be more glorious or rewarding than to die as a martyr for Christ?

It was in this simple faith that Francis planned to become the apostle to the Moslems, but it was some time before he managed to put his plan into operation. The first attempt was made in 1212 but met with disaster. Francis, fully aware of the risks which he ran and, in Celano's words, "burning with the utmost desire for holy martyrdom", took a few of his disciples and set sail, probably from Ancona. Contrary winds, however, drove them on to the coast of Dalmatia and the journey to Syria had to be abandoned. After some difficulty the friars returned to Italy as stowaways and all hope of a voyage to the East in that year was lost.[1] But Francis by no means gave up his intention, and two years later, in 1214, set his face in the opposite direction and embarked on a journey through Spain to Morocco. This expedition, however, also failed, for, while in Spain, Francis was struck down with sickness so severe that the attempt had to be abandoned, and he returned to Italy. When the General Chapter of the Order met in 1217 it was decided to send out missionaries further afield and Francis, on this occasion, set out for France, where, presumably, he hoped to preach among the Albigensians. But again he was stopped, this time by Cardinal Ugolino who met him at Florence and forbade him to cross the Alps.

By this time Francis had been three times thwarted in his attempts to fulfil his mission to the infidels, but still his desire remained, and in 1219 he got his opportunity. When the General Chapter met at Whitsuntide this year it was decided that a further effort should be made to extend the work of the Order overseas and Francis immediately decided to set out again for the East. This time he took about a dozen of the friars with him and they all sailed from Ancona on Midsummer Day. They seem to have touched first at Acre, but went on from there to Damietta which at the time was being besieged by the Christian armies. The friars spent some time with the crusading troops and it was here that Francis received his first shock. In his youthful dreams crusaders had been giants and heroes, endued with all the greatest Christian virtues, dedicated to the service of God, signed with the cross as a mark of their religious zeal. Among the ranks of the troops which he found in Egypt, he met, indeed, a few heroes, but he

[1] 1 *Cel.* 55.

also found many whose lives had little that was Christian about them. There were some adventurers, some fugitives from justice, and a large crowd of hard-swearing, loose-living soldiers whose main object in life was to save their own skins, earn as much pay as they could, and get as much pleasure as was possible out of this hard life. Francis was horrified; his idol was shattered; the ideal which he had cherished from his youth lay soiled and broken at his feet. There was only one thing which he could do; he must denounce them, and leave them to their fate. So, before the assault on the city Francis uttered his solemn warning. It went entirely unheeded; the assault was made; the attackers were hopelessly defeated; and Francis was left to mourn the loss of six thousand men.

Francis saw that, with the morals of the crusading army so low, military success could scarcely be hoped for; and he turned now to the real purpose of his mission, which was the conversion of the Sultan and, through him, of the whole Moslem world. But how was he to reach him? There was only one way; he must walk boldly forward through the Christian lines and demand an interview with the Sultan. How he ever reached the Sultan's presence is a mystery which can never be solved, but there was something about this shabby little man which even the boldest and most reckless found overpowering, and each guard passed him on to the next until Francis, accompanied by the faithful if frightened Brother Illuminato, found himself face to face with Melek-el-Kamil, Sultan of Egypt and leader of the Saracen hosts.

What actually took place in that tent is difficult to say. There are various versions of the story, but that of Bonaventura is probably the most accurate, for he seems to have derived his information from Brother Illuminato who lived until 1273. According to this account the Sultan began by asking the friars who they were and where they came from, to which Francis replied: "We have been sent not by man but by God Most High to show you and your people the way of salvation and to preach the Gospel of Truth." This reply seems to have impressed the Sultan, who invited the friars to stay with him. Francis immediately said that if the Sultan and his people would be converted he would gladly stay with him, but that if he were in doubt let a fire be kindled "and I and your priests will enter the fire, that even so you may learn which faith is the surer, the holier and most worthy of being held". But the Sultan was doubtful whether any of his priests would submit to such an ordeal, especially as one of the most distinguished of them had quietly left the room when Francis made his proposal. So Francis said: "If you will promise me, on behalf of yourself and your people, that you will embrace the faith of Christ if I come forth from the fire unscathed, I will enter the fire alone. If I am burnt, let it be set down to my sins, but if the Divine Might protect me, you shall know that Christ, the Power of God and the Wisdom of God, is the true God and the Lord and Saviour of all."

However, the Sultan would not agree to this proposal, though it is clear that he was deeply impressed by the faith and courage of the saint. He now wished to show his admiration and friendship in the normal oriental way by showering the most expensive presents upon St Francis, all of which, of course, he refused. Even when among his own people he had no interest in worldly goods, how much less could he receive gifts at the hands of an enemy! So he continued to plead for a conversion; but the Sultan, though friendly, was not prepared to abandon the faith of his fathers, and Francis eventually had to accept failure and allow himself to be led back to the camp of the Christians.[1]

Soon after this Francis went on to Palestine for what must have been, in some ways, the most refreshing time of his life. For any Christian to visit the Holy Land and to be able to say "This is the road on which Christ walked: this is the view at which he must often have looked", is a great experience. But to one who lived so near to his Master and who had meditated so long on each detail of his life and teaching, it must have been wonderful indeed. In spite of the failure of his mission to the Christian troops and to the Sultan, in spite

[1] Bon: *Leg. Maj.*, ix, 8f.

of his endless worries about the state of the Order, and in spite of his own ill health, these months in Palestine were, for Francis, a time of real rest and refreshment. But they were brought to a sudden and tragic end by the arrival of Brother Stephen with news from Italy which made Francis leap up from the table at which he was sitting and make immediate arrangements to return home.

In order to understand the sense of urgency which sent Francis rushing back to Italy we must go back a little in our story. In the ten years or so which had elapsed since the coming of the first disciples the little brotherhood had grown into a great religious Order, and the machinery which had proved adequate in the early days, when almost every question was decided by Francis personally, was now proving itself hopelessly inadequate. There was, for example, no means of testing the vocations of those who came to join the Order, no training, no novitiate. Again, the type of life envisaged by St Francis, while suitable enough for a small band of friends, was quite unsuitable for a large Order numbering many thousands of friars. Many of the brethren had never seen St Francis and had only a vague idea of what he stood for or of what his wishes were. Above all, there was no proper Rule. The only Rule was that of 1210, a few texts from the Scriptures strung together with some simple regulations to govern the lives of the brethren. To this a few additions had been made but without any official sanction, and the whole thing was growing more haphazard and chaotic. And still the Order grew.

Francis felt himself losing grip. While he could act as the most inspiring of leaders to a small group of enthusiasts, he was not a great administrator, nor could he direct the affairs of a great religious Order. He depended far too much upon direct personal influence and upon the hour-to-hour guidance of the Holy Spirit. He could not plan ahead because he was never certain where God would lead him, and he could not hope to hold together large numbers of men whom he had never seen and of whose devotion and zeal he had no evidence.

Meanwhile, however, there were others who felt that they could help where Francis knew himself to be helpless, and who could supply the kind of direction and organizing ability which he lacked. Chief among these was the Cardinal Ugolino, Bishop of Ostia, who had the greatest admiration for the saint, had shown much interest in the growth of the Order, and since 1216, had been its Protector. Ugolino was a great ecclesiastical statesman and a future Pope. Passionately keen on Church reform he thought he saw, in the Order of Friars Minor, an instrument which might be used to purify the life of the Church, to inaugurate a great religious revival, and to supplement the work of the parish priests and religious Orders. But if the friars were to be used in this way there must be some organization. At present things were drifting, and no statesman likes drift. There must be a proper plan and a Rule and a basis of government if the Order was to be of any service to the Church. Once that had been done, and the Order was properly on its feet, then there was no end to the amount of good which it might do.

Ugolino opened his mind to St Francis. He explained the plan which he had in mind. The friars were to be brought more into the general policy of the Church. Their poverty and devotion was an example to all and might be used to inspire and elevate the minds of all churchpeople. Then he proceeded to explain that he wished the friars to take a lead in Church affairs. In the early Church it had been poor men who had been chosen leaders, why should not poor men take the lead again? Francis listened attentively but with growing uneasiness. He had founded his brotherhood on the rock of humility. Was this great and good man, with his plans for the Order, aware of what humility meant to them? Wise and noble though he was, did he really understand what Francis was trying to do? And still the Cardinal went on with his schemes and hopes. "Why", he said, "should we not make bishops and prelates of your brethren who excel other men in teaching and example?" But Francis could stand no more. "My Lord," he said, "my brethren are called 'Lesser' just so that they may not aspire to become 'Greater'. Their calling teaches them to live in lowliness, and to follow the footsteps of Christ's humility. . . . If you would have them bear fruit in the Church of God, hold and keep them in the state to which they have been called and bring them back to humility even though it be against their will."[1]

Ugolino had to give in. The time was not yet ripe for that particular scheme, though it came later on. The next attempt was made by some of the friars who approached Ugolino with the request that he would try to persuade Francis to give up his own Rule altogether and adopt one of the existing Rules of the monastic orders. But when Ugolino put this proposal to the saint, Francis replied with considerable vigour: "Brothers, brothers; the Lord has called me by way of Humility, and He has shown me the way of Simplicity; and I do not want you to mention to me any other Rule, neither that of St Augustine, nor of St Benedict, nor of St Bernard. And the Lord told me that He wished me to be a new fool in the world, and that He did not want to lead us by any other way than by that wisdom, for by your learning and your wisdom God will confound you." And so vehement had been Francis' outburst that we are told that "the Cardinal was much amazed and answered nothing, and all the friars feared greatly".[2]

All this happened in 1218 and it is clear that Francis then held the initiative. Plans might be made and schemes proposed, but if Francis did not approve he could still make his will felt. But in the following year he went off to the East, and it was while he was absent from Italy that things began to go wrong. For one thing Ugolino managed to force upon the Poor Clares a set of regulations which were quite out of keeping with the Franciscan ideal, while he also appointed as their visitor a Cistercian monk, a member of the strictest Order then in existence. Then at the General Chapter of 1220 rules about fasting were passed which were also alien to the spirit upon which Francis was trying to build up his fraternity.

[1] 2 Cel. 48.   [2] Spec. 68.

The summer of 1220 was, therefore, a very critical time. Francis was away, and, in his absence, things were happening which his closest friends knew were against his will. The longer Francis was away the more deterioration there would be. So there was only one thing to do: they must get him back. If he were there, he would be able to make his presence felt. So Brother Stephen rushed off to Acre, gave Francis an account of what was happening, and implored him to return. Francis had no doubt as to what he should do. He set sail immediately for Italy.

Francis arrived at Venice about the end of July and made his way to Bologna where the friars had not only built themselves a stone house but were also planning to open a school in connection with the University there. Francis rushed into the house like a whirlwind and sent the friars packing, including some who were sick.[1] Then he went on to the Portiuncula where an extra meeting of the Chapter had been summoned for Michaelmas Day. But if Francis was preparing to make a last bid for liberty the wind was taken out of his sails by a papal bull of 22 September imposing a year's novitiate on all would-be friars. Francis was still, officially, Minister General of the Order, but he felt that the direction of the Order was no longer in his hands and that it was useless to struggle against such mighty powers as were against him. When the Chapter met he abdicated.

The remaining six years of Francis' life (1220-6) were a sad time for him. Absolutely certain of his vocation and of the particular form which it had taken, and longing to get others to accept the same standards of humility and poverty, he was obliged to see more and more departures from the original Rule and intention of the Order, while strong-minded men who failed to share in his ideals got more and more power into their own hands. Francis bore it all with such patience and humility as he could command, but that it was a very sore trial to him is shown by his occasional outbursts both vocal

[1] *Spec.* 6.

and physical. Once he cried out: "Who are they who snatch my Order and my brethren out of my hands? If I come to the General Chapter I'll show them what they will get."[1] And when he once arrived at the Portiuncula and found the friars building a stone building, which was entirely against his wishes, he climbed up on to the roof and began hurling the tiles to the ground with his own hands.

In all this we see a very different Francis from the man whom we met in the stories of the early days. There is here something stern and even violent, a man moved by powerful emotions who could act with sudden passion and rebuke with severity. And yet, though Francis was very deeply moved, and sometimes very angry, in the midst of it all his humility is ever breaking through. "There is no prelate in the whole world", he once said with remarkable insight, "who is so much feared as the Lord would make me to be feared, if I so wished it, by my brethren. But", he added, "the Lord has granted me this grace that I wish to be content with all, as he that is least in the Order."[2] Humility was the greatest of all virtues, but it needed great humility to see your own child which you had borne and cherished, taken into the hands of others who, without knowing it, were undoing much of what you had been trying to do. To arrive, tired and hungry, at a house of the friars and be turned away with curses and blows and left outside in the wet and cold, and to accept this with humility and gladness was a sign of perfect joy; it was far more difficult to count it perfect joy when you stood up before the friars and implored them to stand firm by the high standards of poverty and humility and simplicity, and they only mocked and sneered and ignored what you said. Yet Francis was trying to learn this lesson, for he once said:

> Suppose that, being set over the brethren, I go to the Chapter and preach to them and admonish them, and at the end they speak against me, saying, 'An unlettered and contemptible man will not do for us; therefore we will not have

[1] *Spec.* 41.   [2] *Spec.* 46.

thee to reign over us, because thou art uneloquent, simple and ignorant'; and finally I am expelled with obloquy and despised by them all. I tell thee that unless I heard these words with unchanged looks, with unchanged gladness of mind, and with unchanged purpose of sanctity, I should by no means be a Lesser Brother.[1]

Francis was indeed passing through the furnace, but he had not altogether surrendered his power yet. There was still work to be done, still a battle to be fought for the Lady Poverty and for the ideals of humility and simplicity for which he had always striven. He was not going to desert his love in this hour of peril, however powerful and influential might be the forces against him.

The burning problem in these years was the Rule. Here was a great religious Order with some five or ten thousand members; and yet the only Rule was a simple document which Francis had drawn up when the whole brotherhood consisted of only twelve members and when they had scarcely begun their apostolate.

So Francis spent the winter of 1220-1 in composing a new Rule which was offered to the General Chapter in the following spring and which remained for two years the unofficial Rule of the Order. This document was intended as a compromise and, as so often happens with compromises, it pleased nobody. No one can suppose that it really represents the wishes of St Francis, for it contains a number of concessions which the earlier Rule would never have sanctioned. It relaxes the earlier standard of the single tunic by allowing a friar now to have two habits, one with a hood and one without. It allows the friars to possess books for the purpose of saying the offices, and it makes various allowances for a man who found it difficult to give all his goods to the poor on joining the Order. In some ways, therefore, this new Rule was meant as an offer to the more liberal, relaxing party. But as a peace-offering it

[1] 2 *Cel.* 145.

failed, and Francis knew that further concessions would be demanded before they had done with him.

In 1221 Francis lost one of his best friends, Peter Catanii, who had succeeded him as Minister General and who had helped him in the writing of the latest Rule. His place at the head of the Order was taken by Brother Elias, the man who has had to bear most of the blame for the departure of the Order from its primitive purity. Elias was a great admirer of St Francis, but he was also ambitious, both for the Order and for himself. Of humble origin, he found himself on terms of intimacy with those who held the highest positions in the Church, and to some extent his head was turned by success. In spite of his devotion to the saint it is doubtful whether he ever really understood what Francis was striving for; and, like Ugolino and others, he was anxious to use the immense forces which Francis had generated in order to promote the work of the Church. His appointment as Minister General in 1221 was something of a disaster, for it meant that the relaxing party were now in power and Francis' own will became more and more disregarded.

The first thing was to supersede the Rule of 1221 which those in power regarded as too harsh. So Francis was bidden to write another, and he retired to the wooded hills of Fonte Colombo in the Valley of Rieti with a handful of friends to make one more attempt to solve the problem of how to satisfy the relaxing party and yet be true to his conscience and his ideals. The misery which he endured as he walked through the woods, or sat and meditated in his cave, must have been almost more than he could bear. At last he completed his task and presented it to Honorius III and Cardinal Ugolino. But they found it unacceptable and prevailed on Francis to make certain vital alterations such as the omission of the clause which formed the very basis of the Franciscan way of life: "When the brothers go about the world they are to carry nothing with them."

Pious pilgrims in Franciscan Italy point to Fonte Colombo as the "Sinai" of the Order. But the document which proceeded from that hermitage expresses but a poor shadow of the real wishes of St Francis. "If any man shall come to join the brothers let him sell all his goods and take care to give everything to the poor." So Francis had written in the earliest Rule and so they had done—Francis, and Bernard, and Silvester, and the rest of them. But now, thirteen years later, this clear demand has been whittled down and the postulant is told that "if he cannot do this then his goodwill shall be enough". Again in the primitive Rule the friar is allowed but one tunic with the cord and breeches. This had been enough for the early friars who had borne the cold and discomfort rather than disobey what they regarded as a divine command. But in 1221 a second habit had been permitted, and by 1223 this was increased to include a *caparone* or large cape and sandals.

As soon as the text was complete it was taken to the Pope who confirmed it and sealed it with a Bull on 25 November 1223. The Rule of the Order of Friars Minor was now officially sanctioned; but what the struggle had meant to the sensitive mind and conscience of St Francis who can say? Once the struggle was over he retired to the mountain hermitage of Greccio where he spent the winter and following spring with one or two of his closest friends. While there he spent much time in solitary prayer; "he came not down from his cell except at meal-times and immediately returned thither."[1] During these long hours of meditation he must have thought much of the history of the Order and of the events which had taken place during the last two or three years. His little plant which he had watched over and cared for with such tenderness had been wrenched from his hands. Others were now twisting the Rule to their own ends and had forced him to give up some of his most cherished ideals. And what could he do? He held no official position in the Order; he had no power except his own personality, and for a time he was too sick and too unhappy to attempt to make his influence felt.

Yet he decided to make one last appeal to the brethren. He

[1] *Per.* 66.

would draw up a Will in which he would tell them about the early days and the ideals which they had set before them. If the friars could only know of the joys and pains of those great days when there were but a handful of them and when they gave their all in the service of God and of the Lady Poverty, surely they would not want to abandon the high ideals which they had set themselves! This Testament of St Francis is far the most tender and moving of all the writings of the saint. "Thus did the Lord give to me, Brother Francis, to begin to do penance," it begins, "for when I was in sin it seemed to me very bitter indeed to see lepers; but the Lord Himself led me among them and I showed pity upon them. . . . And then after a little while I came out from the world." A little later he writes of the first friars who came to him, and of their life together, and of how God revealed to them that they were to live according to the precepts of the Gospel. They gave everything which they had to the poor and were satisfied with one habit, patched within and without if they so wished, and the cord and breeches, "and we did not want anything else". Then he tells how they said their prayers, and how they laboured with their hands and begged for alms, and how God revealed to them that they should greet people with the words: "The Lord give you peace." Then he turns from reminiscence to injunction and exhortation, imploring the brothers not to seek privileges and not to depart any further from the way which God had given them. This was his final message to them. He would say no more. It was his last will and testament.[1]

At Greccio Francis tried to find solace and peace. His mind was filled with thoughts of Christ's earthly life as he pictured each scene, and as Christmas drew near he determined to stage a re-enactment of the scene at Bethlehem on the night of Christ's nativity. "There was in that place", says Celano "a man named John, of good repute but of better life, whom the blessed Francis loved with special affection." A fortnight before Christmas Francis sent for him and told him that he

[1] *Opusc.*, pp. 77-82.

wished to "make a memorial of that child who was born in Bethlehem, and in some sort behold with bodily eyes His infant hardships, how he lay in a manger on the hay, with the ox and the ass standing by". So John made the necessary preparations—a stable with the beasts standing there, a manger full of hay, and in the midst an altar where the holy mysteries might be celebrated. And there, in those simple and homely surroundings, at midnight, Mass was said with Francis serving as deacon and reading the Gospel with such devotion that men and women wept with joy.[1] Thus was inaugurated the "Christmas Crib" which is now so loved a feature of our churches at Christmas time.

Francis stayed on at Greccio through Lent and over Easter; but as the days lengthened he determined once more to set out on his travels, though his infirmities were such that often he was unable to move. Never very robust, his health had been deteriorating for a long time. The strain of the hard life which he had led since his conversion, the cold and hunger which he had endured, the constant exposure to rough weather, the persecutions of the early days, the endless journeys and all the self-imposed strains of all-night vigils, scourgings, fastings, and tears had taken heavy toll of his strength. Now his body was racked with disease and he was seldom, if ever, free from pain. Moreover his eyes were beginning to fail him—some say from excessive weeping for the Passion of Christ. But as the world which he had loved so much was gradually taken from his sight his spirit soared to greater love towards God. In the autumn of 1224 he visited St Clare at St Damian's, but he collapsed there and could go no further. A rough hut was made for him in the garden, and there he lay in total darkness for more than sixty days, so weak that he could not drive away the swarms of rats and mice which ran all over him. Yet in all that discomfort and pain his joy rose triumphant, and at last he burst forth into one of the greatest of all Christian hymns, the "Canticle of the Sun".

[1] 1 *Cel.* 84-7.

Most High, Omnipotent Lord,
  Praise, glory and honour be given to Thee with one
                                              [accord!

To Thee alone, Most High, does praise belong,
  Yet none is worthy to make of Thee his song.

Be praised, my Lord, with all Thy works whate'er they be,
  Our noble Brother Sun especially,
  Whose brightness makes the light by which we see,
  And he is fair and radiant, splendid and free,
  A likeness and a type, Most High, of Thee.

Be praised, my Lord, for Sister Moon and every Star
  That thou hast formed to shine so clear from heaven afar.

Be praised, my Lord, for Brother Wind and Air,
  Breezes and clouds and weather foul or fair—
  To every one that breathes Thou givest a share.

Be praised, my Lord, for Sister Water, sure
  None is so useful, lowly, chaste and pure.

Be praised, my Lord, for Brother Fire, whose light
  Thou madest to illuminate the night,
  And he is fair and jolly and strong and bright.

Be praised, my Lord, for Sister Earth our Mother,
  Who nourishes and gives us food and fodder,
  And the green grass and flowers of every colour.

This song Francis taught the friars to sing, and many an
hour of darkness was cheered by the sound of Brother Pacifico
the "King of Verses", singing to him. Once when Francis
heard that there was a violent dispute between the Bishop and
Governor of Assisi he told the friars to go into town and
sing their song, adding an extra verse:

Be praised, my Lord, for those who for Thy love forgive,
    Contented unavenged in quiet to live.
    Blest those who in the way of peace are found—
    By Thee, O Lord Most High, they shall be crowned!

Finally, when Francis knew that he was dying he added one final verse:

Be praised, my Lord, for our Sister Bodily Death,
    From whom none can escape that has drawn breath.
    "Woe to those dying in mortal sin!" He saith.
    Blest those who find that in Thy Holy Will
    The second Death to them will bring no ill.

Praise ye and bless my Lord, and do Him service due,
    With humblest thanks for all He has done for you.[1]

[1] Translation by F. C. Burkitt, *The Song of Brother Sun, in English Rime*, 1926.

6

The Last Years

THOMAS of Celano in his *Second Life of St Francis* has given us an account of the various objects of the saint's special devotions. He begins by telling us that Francis could never hear the expression "the love of God" without going into a kind of rapture, and he then tells us of his special reverence for the angels, for the Mother of Jesus, for the Nativity of Christ, for the Sacrament of the Lord's Body, and for the relics of the saints. But of all the special devotions of the saint that which meant most to him was the Passion of Christ.[1] This had been his constant thought since the day on which the crucifix in St Damian's church had spoken to him and he had turned his mind to contemplate the Crucified. Ever since that day he had made it his ambition to follow Christ in every detail of his life. It was for Christ's sake that he had become poor, that he had humbled himself, that he had worked so hard to preach and to exemplify the Gospel, that he had faced sorrow and anxiety and loneliness. He had tried to obey, to the letter, every known command of Christ, and he had tried to make his own life an "Imitation" of the earthly life of his Saviour. There remained only one path along which he had not been able to follow him, the way of the Cross. He had sought martyrdom in the East and it had been denied him. But as Francis gazed at the Cross he longed to be able to share in the agony which Christ "for us men and for our salvation" had endured, and to be allowed in some way to become a partaker in the Passion of the Redeemer.

In these later years Francis was becoming more and more

[1] *2 Cel.* 196–202.

detached from the affairs of the Order. While other men—Elias and Ugolino and their party—were surrounded by plans and drafts and memoranda for the future of the Order, Francis retired more and more to the solitary places where he could be alone with God, and where he could live, together with a few intimate friends, the life to which he had always believed that God had called them. Among the places which he loved were the rock-hewn hermitages of the Valley of Rieti—Greccio, Fonte Colombo, Poggio Bustone. But of all places the most remote and the most apt for prayer and meditation was the wild summit of the mountain of La Verna.

In the year 1213 Francis, on one of his evangelistic tours, had come to the castle of Montefeltro where he had met a man called Orlando da Chiusi. This man had been so deeply impressed by Francis' preaching and sincerity that he had tried to make him a present. Normally Francis refused all such offers of gifts; but in this case he accepted, for the proposed gift was a mountain-top, and he knew at once that this was what the friars needed as a place of retreat. Thus on 8 May of that year "the said Mount La Verna with all the land whether wooded, rocky or grassy, without any exception, from the brow of the mountain to its foot"[1] was conveyed to the friars for ever.

To this place of retreat Francis bent his steps in the late summer of 1224, taking with him a small party of his closest friends—Leo, Angelo, Masseo, Rufino, Silvester, Illuminato and possibly Bonizzo. When they reached the top of the mountain they built themselves a few little huts out of the branches of trees. At first Francis lived with them, but as he became more and more absorbed in God he found it best to move a little further away. One side of the mountain is composed of jagged rocks, some of which stand up like pinnacles and it was upon the top of one of these that Francis decided to make his retreat. Some logs were, therefore, dragged to the place and a rough bridge made so that access to the rock might be given, and here Francis built himself a tiny cell and retired

[1] *A New Fior.*, p. 79.

to spend the "Lent of St Michael" in solitude. Each night Leo was to bring a little bread and water to the bridge and cry, "O Lord, open thou our lips". If Francis replied "Come" he was to go forward, but if there was no reply he was to return in silence to the place whence he had come. No other person was to cross the bridge on any account.

One night, early in September, when Leo came to the bridge and sang out his versicle there was no reply; but, instead of going back as he had been instructed, he feared for Francis' safety and went forward as far as the little cell. Finding it empty he crept into the wood which surrounded it, and there, in the moonlight, he saw the saint in ecstasy, kneeling among the rocks with his hands uplifted while he repeated over and over again: "Who art thou, my God most sweet? And what am I, thy unprofitable servant and vilest of worms?" Then, as Leo crouched down in awe and wonder, what he described as a flaming torch descended from heaven and rested for a while on the head of St Francis before it returned to the sky. When all was over Leo turned to creep back, but Francis heard him and admonished him for having been disobedient and having crossed the bridge.

The incident had certainly frightened Leo very much. Like Peter and James and John he had seen his master transfigured, and he knew that things were happening between Francis and God which no man would ever fully understand. He returned in fear and trembling to his companions, and the little party waited anxiously, knowing that strange events were taking place on their mountain-top, while their thoughts and their prayers were constantly with their beloved leader on his lonely rock.

They had not very long to wait, for on Holy Cross Day, 14 September, the vigil reached its climax. Very early on that morning, when it was still dark, Francis had been praying under the stars. "O my Lord, Jesus Christ," he said, "two graces do I pray thee to grant unto me before I die: the first, that while I live I may feel in my body and in my soul, so far as is possible, that sorrow, sweet Lord, that thou didst suffer in the hour of thy most bitter passion; the second, that I may feel in my heart, so far as may be possible, that exceeding love wherewith, O Son of God, thou wast enkindled to endure willingly for us sinners agony so great." Then, when his prayer was ended, there appeared to him a vision of the Crucified in a light so brilliant and dazzling that people in the neighbouring villages thought that the sun had risen and started on their day's work. This glow lasted for over an hour while Francis remained in an ecstasy of joy and wonder. When at last the light waned and the vision faded, Francis discovered, in his hands and his feet and side, wounds like those of the crucified Christ whom he loved so dearly and whose passion he had longed to share.[1]

How these wounds came upon his body no man will ever know, but of their presence there was never the slightest doubt, though Francis did his very best to keep them secret. He knew that a great miracle had been wrought in him, but he feared greatly that a privilege so personal and so mysterious should be exploited and therefore he should become a spectacle to the world. He therefore saw that his hands and feet were always covered, and was constantly on his guard against the discovery of his secret. Nevertheless, several of the friars began to have their suspicions, and some of them tried, by various means, to discover the truth. Brother Rufino, for example, once put his hand into the saint's bosom to scratch him and in so doing his hand slipped and touched the scar.[2] Another friar by chance saw the wounds in Francis' feet and cried out: "What is this, good brother?" to which the saint replied: "Mind your own business." The same friar once asked Francis if it was blood that he saw on his habit, and the saint put his finger to his eye and said: "If you don't know that to be an eye, you'd better ask what it is."[3] So, with the utmost care, Francis tried to conceal the stigmata which he bore, though it was almost impossible to do so. Yet the secret seems to have been well kept; for those who suspected or who believed that they knew

[1] *Fior.*, "Consideration of the Stigmata". [2] 1 *Cel.* 95.
[3] 2 *Cel.* 135f.

the truth appear to have honoured the saint's desire that the affair should not become public property, and, except for one or two who knew, Francis was able to carry his secret to the grave.

But on the night of Francis' death Elias, as Minister General, wrote an open letter in which he described the appearance of the saint's body. "And now", he wrote, "I make known to you a great joy and a new thing among miracles. From the beginning of the world no such sign has been heard of, except in the Son of God, who is Christ. Not long before his death our brother and father appeared as one crucified, bearing in his body five wounds which are the very stigmata of Christ. For his hands and his feet had as it were the holes of nails, pierced through on both sides, remaining as wounds and having the blackness of nails. His side also seemed to be pierced, and often bled."[1] There are other descriptions, but none so authentic as this, written perhaps with the body actually before the eyes of the writer.

When Francis had seen the vision of the Crucified, and had discovered the prints of the wounds on his body, he knew that his vigil on La Verna could now be brought to an end, and he left his solitary rock and returned, racked with pain, to his disciples. Preparations were now made to leave the mountain-top, but, before they left, Francis took pen and ink and with his wounded hand wrote down a hymn in praise of the Crucified. Then he turned the parchment over, and on the back, he inscribed, for Brother Leo's benefit, the Aaronic blessing:

The Lord bless thee and keep thee:
The Lord make his face to shine upon thee and be gracious
    unto thee:
The Lord lift up the light of his countenance upon thee
    and give thee peace.

Then, under that, he wrote: "The Lord bless, Brother Leo, thee"; and then he drew the sign of the cross. This piece of

[1] *A New Fior.*, p. 80f.

parchment he gave to his friend and disciple, and Leo carried it in his bosom until his death. It is now in the sacristy of the Church of St Francis at Assisi, still showing the creases where Leo folded it up and placed it near his heart.

At the end of September the party prepared to descend from the hill-top, but Francis was too weak and too severely wounded to be able to walk, and an ass was, therefore, brought upon which he might ride. Thus, slowly and not without great pain, the little cavalcade made its way down the steep hill-side. It was an early winter and snow was already falling. So slowly did they progress that once they were unable to reach the village and were obliged to spend a whole night sheltering under a rock while the snow fell all around them. Slowly they made their way south, through Borgo San Sepolcro and Citta di Castello, following the course of the Tiber, until at last they reached the little church of the Portiuncula where, for a while, Francis was able to rest. But his ardent spirit was still yearning to do more for Christ, and it is recorded that he once cried out: "Brothers, let us begin to serve the Lord God, for hitherto we have profited little or nothing", while he even thought that he would be able to go back to the leper-houses and serve the lepers.[1] But his body was so weak with disease and pain that he could scarcely move and this eventually persuaded him to give up any idea of further work and to submit to some kind of medical treatment, especially for his eyes. Elias knew of a surgeon at Rieti who might be able to do something to relieve the pain, and thither he set off with St Francis as winter drew on.

The first day they got only as far as St Damian's and here Francis had to rest for more than eight weeks, during the whole of which he was totally blind. Then in February 1225 they managed to go on to Rieti where a lay friend kindly put them up in his house. As Francis lay there in pain and darkness he suddenly conceived the idea that he would like to hear some music, so he called one of the friars who had been a lute-player before he joined the Order, and bade him borrow a lute and

[1] 1 Cel. 103f.

sing to him. But the poor friar, torn between love of St Francis and, perhaps, fear of Elias, asked to be excused since he was afraid that the people of the town would criticize him. So Francis let the matter drop. "But", says Brother Leo,

> the following night, about midnight, Francis was lying awake, and lo, close to the house where he lay, he heard a minstrel playing the sweetest music which he had ever heard in the whole of his life. And as he played he went up and down, going first so far away as to be almost inaudible and then coming back, but always playing. And this continued for a full hour. Wherefore the blessed Francis, knowing that this was a work of God, not of man, was filled with the greatest joy and with gladness of heart praised God with all his strength in that He had been pleased to cheer his soul with such consolation.[1]

Francis had come to Rieti in order to have some treatment for his eyes and preparations were now made for the operation. The method was that of cauterization, which meant the burning with a hot iron of his face from the jaw to the eyebrow with the purpose apparently of "opening the veins". It sounds barbaric to us, but in those days was thought to be efficacious, and the surgeon really believed that it would eventually relieve the pain. Francis submitted because Brother Elias wished it and had taken great trouble to prepare for it, but even his gallant spirit quailed when he saw the iron put into the fire to be heated up. For a moment he thought he would faint, but, summoning all his strength, he addressed the fire in these words: "My Brother Fire, noble and useful among all other creatures, be kind to me in this hour, for I have always loved thee for the love of Him who created thee. But I pray our Creator who created us, that He will so temper thy heat that I may be able to bear it." Then he made the sign of the cross over the fire and the surgeon took the red-hot iron and plunged it into the flesh. The sight was so terrible that all

[1] Per. 59; cf. 2 Cel. 126.

the friars who were present fled from the room, but when they returned Francis reproved them for their lack of courage and assured them that he had felt no pain whatsoever.[1]

Needless to say, this rough treatment did no good, and Francis was at length carried away from Rieti to Siena where there were known to be good physicians who might be able to give him some relief. Elias was deeply concerned for his master and went to infinite trouble to obtain the best possible treatment for him, but it was Leo, Masseo, Angelo, and Rufino who remained with the saint and nursed him in his sickness. He was not an easy patient. Whenever the friars managed, sometimes with great difficulty, to get him some food which he could swallow, or some bed-clothes to keep him warm, Francis almost invariably managed to give them away, thinking of all kinds of dodges to deceive his attendants. Yet he was aware that he was causing them great anxiety and much work, for he once said to them: "Dearest brothers, and my little children, let it not weary you to labour for my infirmity, for the Lord will pay back to you all the fruit of your works for His humblest servant in this world and in the next."[2]

The party stayed at Siena through the winter of 1225-6, but it gradually became clear that the doctors could do nothing for their patient and that it was really only a question of giving him as much comfort as possible until the end. In addition to the trouble with his eyes he was now suffering greatly from internal weakness, causing hæmorrhages and much pain, and then dropsy developed. Besides this there was the constant pain from the wounds in his hands and feet and side. So he lay, month after month, in pain so great that when one of the brethren asked him which he would rather have to endure, this sickness, "so lingering and so long" or the most terrible martyrdom, he replied: "That, my son, ever has been and is dearest, sweetest, and most acceptable to me which it most pleases the Lord my God to do in me and with me. . . . But compared with any kind of martyrdom it would be more

<hr />

[1] *Spec.* 115.   [2] *Spec.* 89.

distressing to me to bear this sickness, were it but for three days."[1]

In the spring of 1226 Elias came to Siena and Francis rallied enough to be carried as far as Celle di Cortona where he remained for few weeks. But it was clear that he was dying, and, by his own special wish, preparations were made to carry him to Assisi so that he could die at his beloved Portiuncula, the spot where his spiritual rebirth had taken place. Elias now took command, managing everything with his accustomed efficiency. He knew that he had taken charge of a very precious burden, and that it was essential to get him safely to Assisi so that eventually the shrine might be built there. Realizing that attempts might be made to seize the frail body, dead or alive, and carry it away to some other place, he arranged for an armed escort of knights to protect the litter and he chose a route which would avoid taking them through Perugia.

Francis had once told the Bishop of Assisi that if he and his followers allowed themselves to have money they would need arms to protect it; but now armed men had been called in to protect him in his poverty and weakness. There is something terribly ironical in this picture of a man who had gone fearlessly among robbers and wolves, who had boldly made his way into the camp of the Saracen hosts, but who must now be watched day and night lest his poor, broken body should be stolen or torn to pieces by relic hunters. But Brother Elias knew what he was doing; he knew the dangers and he knew also the value of the treasure he was carrying.

When they reached Assisi, Francis was taken to the bishop's palace. This being a strongly built house, within the walls of the city, and easily defensible, was thought a safe place in which to deposit the precious burden; and here Francis lay for some weeks. In spite of the terrible pain and discomfort he seems to have found a measure of peace at last, for when one of the brethren reminded him of the way in which the Order was falling away from the ideals which he had set and asked

[1] 1 *Cel.* 107.

him why he did not make his influence felt in stopping the rot, Francis replied that though in the early days he had managed to lead the friars and hold them together by his preaching and by his example, yet, when the number got too big, he had deliberately resigned his position believing that others would be more effective than he could be. If, however, the friars asked him again to be their leader he would gladly do what he could until death separated him from them, but, unless they invited him, he was not going to be "an executioner, punishing and flogging them like the magistrates of this world".[1]

After years of terrible distress, when Francis' spirit had sometimes been almost broken by the defection of the Order, it seems that he had now sailed into calmer waters and was able to detach himself more and more from the events which were taking place around him and to wait quietly for the coming of Sister Death. During the summer a doctor from Arezzo came to see him and the saint asked him how long he had to live. The doctor hedged, but at last said that he thought Francis would die at the end of September or early in October. On hearing this Francis "spread out his hands to the Lord with very great devotion and reverence, and said with great joy of mind and body: 'Welcome, Sister Death.' "[2]

He became happier than ever when he knew that he had not long to wait, and calling in some of the friars he bade them sing the Praises which he had composed. Gathered round the bed the brethren lifted up their voices and sang their hymn:

Most High, Omnipotent, Good Lord,
Praise, glory and honour be given to Thee with one
     accord!

and as their voices rose and fell Francis found peace and comfort. But Elias was horrified. A saint singing as he dies! This was intolerable! So he came to Francis and implored him to stop this scandal, telling him that the people of the town

---

[1] *Spec.* 71.   [2] *Spec.* 122.

would be horrified and would lose their respect for a man who could sing songs when he ought to be thinking of death. But for once Francis refused to obey. "Allow me, brother," he cried, "to rejoice in the Lord, both in His praises and in my infirmities; since, by the grace of the Holy Spirit, I am so united and joined to my Lord that by His mercy I may well rejoice in the Most High."[1] Elias was helpless and retired in distress. But the singing went on.

> Be praised, my Lord, for our Sister Bodily Death
> From whom none can escape that has drawn breath. . . .
> Praise ye and bless my Lord, and do Him service due,
> With humblest thanks for all He has done for you.

By September it was clear that the end could not be far off and Francis asked to be carried down the hill to the Portiuncula. He had one more appointment with Lady Poverty and that was not one which could be made in the palace of a bishop. But the poor little Portiuncula with its circle of rude huts was a fitting place for the lover of poverty to meet his bride and fall asleep in her arms. A litter was therefore procured and the failing body, torn and racked with disease and pain, was carried down the track to the plain. Half-way down the hill Francis bid them halt and turn his face towards the town. His eyes were now sightless but in his mind he could picture the city which he had known and loved, and, while the friars supported him in their arms, he gave it his blessing.

When they reached the Portiuncula they placed the saint in one of the little wooden huts close to the church. He felt happier here in surroundings which, though he could not see them, were familiar, while the poverty and simplicity of the place cheered his spirit. On 30 September, thinking that he was dying, he asked the friars to strip him and lay him naked on the floor in order that he might die in the most abject poverty with nothing that he could call his own. This they did, but he recovered a little and the warden was able to persuade him to take back his clothes—the tunic and breeches

[1] *Spec.* 121.

and the little sackcloth cap which he had worn since the cauterization of his head—saying, with remarkable wisdom and insight: "Know that this tunic, these breeches and this cap have been lent to thee by me on holy obedience." Then Francis rejoiced, knowing, as Celano says, "that he had kept faith with the Lady Poverty even unto the end".[1]

Then the friars were brought in and Francis spoke to them about poverty and patience and the observance of the teaching of Christ. After this he asked them to bring him some bread and, having blessed it, he gave to each a portion as his Master had done in the Upper Room. Then he laid his thin and wounded hands on the head of each friar and gave him his blessing.

The next day or two found him growing steadily weaker, and on the evening of 3 October it was clear that the end was at hand. Francis again asked them to lay him naked in the dust, and, as he lay there, tired and helpless but full of joy and hope, one of the friars, at his special request, read to him from the thirteenth chapter of St John's Gospel: "Now before the feast of the Passover, when Jesus knew that his hour was come that he should depart out of this world unto the Father, having loved his own which were in the world, he loved them unto the end." As the familiar words were read out to him he fell asleep in Christ, while a flock of larks, his favourite birds, gathered round the hut and rose singing into the still evening air.

"Having loved his own which were in the world, he loved them unto the end" or "to the uttermost". These were probably the last words which Francis heard on earth. He too had loved—loved God and loved man with a love of peculiar intensity and recklessness. It was love that had made him leap off his horse and kiss the foul and rotting hand of the leper; it was love that had made him abandon for ever the comforts and decencies of his father's house; it was love which had led him by the way of poverty and humility and simplicity. Love

[1] 2 Cel. 215.

had driven him on his long journeys in heat and cold, in hunger and thirst; love led him to face almost certain death at the hands of the Saracens; love took him up to the mountain-top to be branded as Christ's. His whole life had been nothing but an expression of love—love of God and love of man—to the end, and to the uttermost.

Love of such quality has no object but to rejoice the heart of the Beloved, but the love which Francis showed has had the effect of drawing many to a greater knowledge and love of Christ. In this Francis would have rejoiced, knowing that this love had been used by God.

Some early scribe, having made a collection of stories about St Francis, gave it the title of *The Mirror of Perfection*. This title shows some genius, for it is just what Francis would have wished to be called. A mirror gives no light of its own; all it can do is to reflect the light of others. Francis had tried to reflect something of the glorious light which is in the face of Jesus Christ and so to make it easier for men to know Christ and his will. In the clear light which was given to him he was able to see, as few men have ever seen, "what things he ought to do", and by the grace of God he had been able "faithfully to fufil the same".

Shortly before his death, as he lay naked on the bare ground and looked back over his life, he said to the brethren: "I have done my duty; may Christ teach you yours."[1] From that date onwards many that have been struggling to do their duty have been glad of the "Mirror of Perfection", that holy example of faithfulness and love which we find in the life of St Francis of Assisi.

[1] *2 Cel.* 214.

A Note on Books

The literature about St Francis is vast, but the following notes will give some idea of the most important books in English.

Of the early sources the most important is the collection of St Francis's own writings. Much the best edition of these is *The Writings of St Francis of Assisi*, translated by B. Fahy with introduction and notes by P. Hermann (Burns & Oates 1963). Five of the early Legends about St Francis were published in English translations in the *Temple Classics* early in the present century. These are: *The Converse of Francis and his Sons with Holy Poverty*; *The Legend of the Three Companions*; *The Mirror of Perfection*; the *Life* by St Bonaventura; and *The Little Flowers of Saint Francis*. The last three of these were reprinted in one volume in the Everyman Library. The only important sources not included in this collection were the two *Lives* by Thomas of Celano. These were published in an English version by A. G. Ferrers Howell. *A New Fioretti*, edited by J. R. H. Moorman (SPCK 1946), is a collection of early stories about St Francis from various sources which had not previously been translated.

A very useful modern book is *Saint Francis of Assisi: His Life and Writings as recorded by his Contemporaries*, translated by Leo Sherley-Price (Mowbray 1959). This contains a good translation of *The Mirror of Perfection*. There are, of course, very many translations of *The Little Flowers*. Otto Karrer's *St Francis of Assisi: the Legends and Lauds* (Sheed & Ward 1947) contains translations of some of the sources.

All the above (with the exception of the material collected in *A New Fioretti*), together with some other early matter, are now obtainable in *Saint Francis of Assisi: Writings and*

117

Early Biographies—English Omnibus of the Sources for the Life of St Francis, edited by Marion A. Habig (Chicago 1973). This is an extremely handy volume, though rather expensive. It also contains a bibliography which is a selection from that recently drawn up by Raphael Brown (see below).

A great many Lives of St Francis have been written, especially in the last eighty years or so since Sabatier published his *Vie de Saint François* in 1894. This has been translated into English and should certainly be read. Less poetical but more accurate is Fr Cuthbert's *St Francis of Assisi* (Longmans) which probably remains the best Life so far produced for the English reader. There is also a good biography by the Danish writer, J. Jörgensen, which has also been translated (Longmans). In addition to these there are about sixty modern Lives of St Francis of very varied importance. G. K. Chesterton's is the most brilliant, though it is full of inaccuracies (Hodder 1960).

The best modern Life is by Omer Englebert, translated by Eve Marie Cooper (1965), containing the comprehensive 'Research Bibliography' of Raphael Brown which covers over a hundred pages. Other modern Lives are by Elizabeth Goudge (Duckworth 1968), Michael de la Bedoyère (Collins 1962), E. M. Almedingen (Bodley Head 1967) and John Holland Smith (Sidgwick & Jackson 1972). There are also a great many smaller books.

Those interested in the subsequent history of the Order of Friars Minor should consult one or more of the following: *A History of the Franciscan Order from its Origins to the Year 1517* by John R. H. Moorman (OUP 1968), *Franciscan Poverty* by M. D. Lambert (SPCK 1961), and *Early Franciscan Government* by Rosalind Brooke (CUP 1959).

The above list is only a fraction of the literature available, but many of the books mentioned provide bibliographies which will give suggestions for those who wish to pursue their studies further.